The Evolution of Love

How a new Paradigm Eliminates Fear so we can Love Openly

Douglas A. McWilliams

ISBN10:1540343715
ISBN 13: 9781540343710

Table of Contents

Introduction

It was an overwhelming desire to help others with their relationships that motivated me to finally publish this book, but the project initially began out of a desire to help myself have better, longer-lasting relationships, and to find a way to minimize the emotional pain to the women that I still cared deeply for when I decided that our romantic relationship should come to an end.

In terms of how we think about and practice love, I don't believe there is a "right" answer that works for everyone; there are only different perspectives, and I feel an intense obligation to share my own perspective.

My views on love and relationships have been shaped over many years, many relationships, many breakups, many conversations, and many hours of intense contemplation. In quiet moments, my mind would constantly ponder the puzzle of love, sex, and relationships. These topics have been an obsession of mine for many years.

My perspective challenges conventional thinking and conventional practice, but *it allows me to approach love and relationships fearlessly*. I have no fear of rejection. I have no fear of heartbreak. I have no fear of being cheated on. What's more, my perspective allows me to fully experience and appreciate love while it is in my life. I started to hash out my ideas about relationships and love many years ago. I felt that there must be a better way to view these issues that would allow us to enjoy happier, and healthier relationships.

I honestly believe that my insights and perspectives will help others understand themselves better, come to a deeper understanding of love, overcome the fear of falling in love, the pain of previous heartbreaks, and get back on the road to loving fully, as we were divinely intended. What are we here for, if not to love others?

In order to find successful, happy relationships, I believe we need to dissect and examine the meaning of the word "love," because it's clear to me that it means different things to different people. As we examine and contrast these two concepts of love, and how they relate to our psychology, we will start to see a new paradigm emerge----a new way to think about and approach relationships, so we can love openly. Without fear.

My insights are largely based on my own experiences and philosophies, but they are also based on science. When I was a younger man, I was reluctant to learn about the science of falling in love, because I had some vague notion that understanding love would dampen or cheapen the magic of the experience. I imagine many feel, the same way. But it is crucial to understand the science of love in order to eliminate the confusion, heartache, disappointment, and ultimately the fear of falling in love. We cannot fully give love or enjoy someone else's love if we fear being hurt by the experience. When we truly understand love, we realize it's nothing to fear, and there is no reason to withhold it; love can never hurt us. The truth is, no one else has the power to break our heart. We break our own heart by failing to comprehend the nature of love, and our complex nature and emotions. Thus, we set unreasonable expectations of our relationships.

Who will benefit from this book? This book should help anyone who is feeling confused about love, sex, and relationships. Its's also written for anyone who is wondering whether marriage is right for them----fewer and fewer younger people today are choosing to get married, and I understand why. For these people, I want to help give them a healthy way to think about and approach to dating so that they may find truly satisfying relationships. This book is also written for anyone who may be emotionally scarred because of a failed marriage or a painful breakup, perhaps even if it's a breakup from the distant past. It is essential to mend the scars from our past if we are going to live and love *fully* in the present. It's also meant for anyone who may be feeling dissatisfied or disillusioned in their current relationship or marriage. Although this book primarily focuses on relationships with a significant other, I also share some thoughts about how we can improve the way people love their friends and family, their neighbors, and the world.

As you read this, I want you to realize something: **you are someone that I care about**. Sincerely. I don't need to know anything about you to care about you and wish you love and happiness in life. Your happiness makes me happy. That is why I am sharing this book for free. If it is helpful to you, and you want to pay something for it, you can go to **www.douglasmcwilliams.com** and you can give a gift for whatever you think it is worth. My book is about love, and I give it as an act of love. This is how love works: <u>you give it first without expecting anything in return</u>. I want people to read this book, because I know it can help strengthen their relationships and live happier lives. I wouldn't feel good about charging money upfront, knowing what it can do to help people. I've tried to keep it as concise as possible, while still hitting the major points I felt necessary.

If we can improve our understanding of love, and improve the way we talk about it, then we can bring more of it into the world. We can improve the quality of our lives, and the lives of those around us.

Chapter 1

<u>Fear</u>

This book is about love, but it's also about *fear*, and the inverse relationship between the two. To whatever extent we have a fear of heartbreak, or being cheated on…we cannot fully give or experience love. I would argue that the same is true about life itself: to whatever degree we have fear in our life, to an inverse degree we are not *fully* experiencing or appreciating life. I find it a great shame that so many are afraid to fall head over heels in love for fear of getting hurt. This fear either keeps us on the sidelines, afraid to pursue relationships, or, if we do pursue relationships, this fear inevitably undermines the quality of our relationships, sabotaging them and shortening their duration.

The fear that we will be hurt and disappointed in our relationships becomes a self-fulfilling prophecy. I've been through it myself, and it took me a long time to overcome. When we are madly in love with someone, it can be scary…like a wild car ride through a mountain pass, and we're unsure if the breaks work! It is exhilarating, but scary. If we are going to open up to love fully and actually enjoy our relationships, then we must remove this fear. Let's begin the journey.

I hope that my comparison of falling in love to being a "wild car ride" resonated with you. But let's think about this…are our fears justified? In the example of the car ride, there is real physical danger in the experience. If we crash or go over the side of the mountain we could be seriously injured or killed. It's logical that our minds would swell with fear. But what is it that we are afraid of when we fall in love? Logically we know that we aren't going to die if the relationship doesn't work out. We aren't going to lose an arm and a leg. Most of will say that we are afraid of the pain that comes with heartbreak, but <u>we need to mature and recognize this is nothing to be afraid of.</u>

Let's consider the phrase, "madly in love". The term "madly" implies that our emotions are so strong that all of our reasoning and logic is out the window. We need change our way of thinking. We must find a way to bring logic and reasoning into our romantic relationships and, once we do, we will be well on our way to mastering our fears.

When we understand the nature of love, we realize that it we actually have nothing to fear from falling in love. My goal is to get you to take that wild car ride of love with abandon! To enjoy the ride, and have the time of your life! I'm confident that I can help reduce the fear, if not eliminate it, improve your relationships. I can help men and women heal previous hurts, and help them get back in the game of love and life; for the two go hand-in-hand.

If we can get past the fear of heartbreak, then we can have happier, more satisfying, and longer lasting relationships. When we remove the fear, it frees us love fully; we realize there is no reason to hold back from feeling or expressing love. We can dive into relationships with abandon, knowing that whatever the outcome is…we're going to be okay. We can love 100% and know that if the other person leaves, finds someone else, or even cheats, it's not going to devastate us, or get us down.

I believe this is possible for everyone. My insights about human nature and my perspectives on love and relationships has freed me from all fear, which is why I feel compelled to share my views and philosophies.

I'm going to attack the problem of fear from several angles. We can start to reduce our fear by simply recognizing the long odds that we face in finding a truly great fit, personality-wise, with any one person; no matter how attracted we may be to them physically. With any new relationship, we must be clear-eyed and recognize: this relationship is *probably not* going to have all of the qualities that we each require to be truly happy together for the rest of our lives. Realizing this reality at the outset of any relationship goes a long way toward reducing fear. I'm just applying logic. We might be extremely attracted to someone, but we have to be aware that there are a lot of other factors that are going to determine whether we are going to be a good match with any one person. It's fine to be hopeful and optimistic, but it is *crucial* to also be realistic about the fact that, most likely, we are not going to be a great match for each other. I use the word *great*, rather than *good*, because I believe our relationships should be great! I think we should all have a goal of having great relationships.

We have a society that is so afraid of heartbreak that many people have soured and given up on love. A notion that is often reinforced by popular music:

"What's love got to do with it? What's love but a secondhand emotion?" --Tina Turner

"Uh oh, uh oh…falling in love, falling in love again" —Miami Sound Machine

People find it scary and difficult to open up and feel love…to show and express love openly. Fear keeps us closed off, but love can only flow in and out of us if we are open. I think one of the major factors that has contributed to the prevailing fear is that we have heard the message time and again since we were children: "be careful who you give your love away to, because they could break your heart." We have to change this kind of thinking, and that is my mission in writing this book. I hope that by the end of this book you no longer see the merits of being "careful with your heart". I want you to understand love as I do, so that no one can ever really hurt you, and you can love recklessly and fearlessly!

I also want to challenge the prevailing idea that love is a limited resource that you should "save" or "reserve" for "one special person" who "truly deserves it." Love is a limitless resource, and everyone deserves our love. Love is not weakened or diluted by extending it to more and more people. Our happiness and sense of well-being grow as we grow to love more and more people, and we become more connected with the world. There is no reason to hold back our love.

Chapter 2

"The Imposter"

Before I ever had a thought to write about love and relationships, I spent a lot of time pondering: how is it that I am able to love fearlessly and openly, without fear of being hurt, where as so many others are not? One thing became very clear to me right away: the popular notion of what love is all about, and how people talk about it, in many ways did not match my definition of love. By the term "popular notion" I'm referring to the depictions, phrases, and concepts about love that we get from popular culture: popular music in particular, but also television and movies, and magazines, and the way people talk about their relationships on Facebook or in public. It seemed to me that this popular notion of love was some kind of imposter. So where did this notion come from?

I quickly realized there are many, many cliché terms and phrases that reflect a gross misunderstanding of love, by my definition. Here are some of the primary examples that stick out from popular music. See if any of these sound familiar:

"I need you"

"You are my reason for living"

"The first time I saw you I knew I wanted you to be mine"

"I will do anything for you"

"All the love I have is for you"

*"I know that you are **the one**"*

"I was nothing before I met you, and you saved me,"

"Will our love stand the test of time?

"I can't live without you"

"I'll never let you go"

"You said you love me, but now you are leaving…I guess you were just using me"

"Go ahead and walk out the door, but you won't find love as good as mine, and someday you're going to be all alone with no one to turn to."

These clichés span the decades. In my opinion, none of these statements has anything to do with love; at least not my concept of love. I think it's time we retire these clichés once and for all. They are not of service to how we comprehend or express love. The ideas and concepts about love and relationships that we hear in pop culture have infiltrated our collective psyche, and they make us confused and fearful of love. I will come back to examine some of these clichés after I define my concept of love, the new paradigm. And I will explain why they do not align with my definition of love.

Why have we accumulated and regurgitated these phrases for so long? I believe that songwriters usually aim to stir people's emotions, rather than attempt to present logical, levelheaded and mature viewpoints. With messages like these echoing in our ears for so long, it's no wonder that we have issues with our relationships. These messages are especially harmful for children and teenagers who haven't had enough real-world experience with love to develop their own concepts. The result is a society of people who are needy, co-dependent, confused, and ultimately fearful of love.

Let me be clear: I'm not judging anyone---not the songwriters, nor anyone who doesn't have an issue with these messages about love. My goal is to help. A life of greater happiness and love awaits us if we can deepen our understanding of love, and improve the way we think and talk about it.

I've cited a lot of examples from pop music, but I see similar issues with the portrayal of love in movies and television. Since this pop culture version of love was so vastly different than my concept of love, I didn't want to call it 'love' at all. I had to come up with another label----I decided to label the pop culture version of love as "the imposter." This "imposter love" is accompanied by feelings of possessiveness, co-dependency, neediness, and, should the relationship end, jealousy, spite, hate, and sometimes the desire to inflict mental or physical harm. Does this sound familiar? How many love songs focus on these selfish and possessive emotions and thoughts? Our concepts and understanding of what it means to love are heavily influenced by our culture…the way we hear others talk about it and describe it. This has real consequences for people's lives and relationships, and our society. We must do better.

It seems to me that the poets, songwriters and movie-makers parading this imposter around (like the Emperor in his suit of "new clothes") as the greatest connection that two people can have, telling us having it makes life "complete" …yet becomes devastating when it's gone and produces negative, destructive emotions. Right from the start of this project I recognized the influence that popular culture has had on creating and perpetuating this "imposter", but I also realized there must be a deeper explanation for the existence of this imposter. I started to ponder human biology and human nature.

The next step in constructing my theory was to consider evolutionary psychology; taking into account that our species has evolved over time. I had to incorporate "survival of the fittest", and think about how the realities that our ancestors faced helped to shape the way we behave and think today. As I thought about humankind's biological drive to procreate and the drive to protect one's offspring, I realized that these possessive and selfish emotions were totally understandable, and useful.

Let us imagine the life of a man of 10,000 years ago. Nature's law of "survival of the fittest" would mean that his brain would be hardwired with certain emotional responses, that would linger in modern humans as well. I think we all know this, but it's important to remind ourselves. Instinctively a man would desire to not only find and impregnate a suitable mate, but also want to make sure that his offspring would grow up to be viable adults that would then find their own mates. Naturally a man would feel possessive of the mate he had chosen and also be jealous and angry (perhaps even to the point of physical violence) if another man was competing for the woman he had chosen as his mate. Naturally, a woman of 10,000 years ago would get quite jealous and possessive should another woman show interest in the man that she chose to be her mate. A man would instinctively want to make sure that the mother of his children stayed home to raise those children and focus on those children rather than run off and start a family with someone else; and a woman would instinctively want to make sure that the father did his part to provide for and protect her offspring. Our genes, in their quest to be replicated and passed on, are powerful drivers of human psychology and behavior. Although they are powerful, we need not be slaves to them. We can rise above them, but we must first acknowledge their presence, and their power.

The drive to find a mate and reproduce is extremely powerful, and it's a good thing that it is so powerful; otherwise none of us would be here today! Every one of our ancestors had to live to be old enough to become sexually reproductive, successfully find a mate, and live to be old enough to ensure that the offspring lived to reach sexual maturity and repeat the process… all the way back to the first life on Earth. To me, this is a staggering thought, and a reason to be extremely grateful to be alive. But it also hammers home the point that the urge to mate is extremely powerful. We all recognize this on some level, but we don't seem to acknowledge it often enough. As a society, we are often very quick to judge others for misjudgments in their sexual relations. I think that's worth pointing out just how powerful our sexual instincts are.

There was a line I read in a book many years ago that struck me like a bolt of lightning, and has stuck with me ever since. I recognized it was a profound statement about the human condition. The line read: "for all of humankind's noble ambitions and lofty ideals, we can never escape the *indelible stamp of our lowly origins.*" I thought it was brilliant, but for years I found the thought a bit depressing: was it true that we could never escape our lowly impulses from our lowly origins? This is the challenge that humanity faces.

I realize now that growth only comes through struggle, and each of us must struggle to overcome those base and selfish impulses. We don't have to be perfect, but we must make the effort to be better. That's life. This is a central concept to the theory I'm about to lay out.

We don't want or need to escape *all* of our primitive emotions and impulses. We don't need to become Mr. Spock from Star Trek and be completely stoic. What we should do is strive to overcome the destructive *negative* emotions that rise up within us. In order to do this, it's absolutely critical to understand that we have evolved from lower organisms.

We must also understand why our brains evolved, and how they currently function because of those evolutionary changes. Those selfish, primal emotional impulses still reside within our modern brain, but they need not rule our state of mind nor rule our behavior. Our primitive impulses can be dispelled and overcome with the power of our conscious mind. We must first understand where these emotions stem from and acknowledge their power and potency. We must not feel guilty for having those impulses; that only makes them harder to vanquish…never underestimate your foe. The next step to is realize that our evolved, conscious minds (which are a more responsible driver of our behavior), can overpower those primitive impulses, should we deem them illogical or not beneficial. This is the first step to getting our emotions in check so that we are no longer slaves to them.

Chapter 3

Primitive Love

I realized that the possessive, selfish, jealous feelings that we still associate with love, that I had labeled "the imposter," could more accurately be labeled "primitive love." Basically, this is a primitive version of love that we all experience as animals, that is essentially the same experience other animals have when they find a mate.

At this point I need to get into the semantics of love. We have so many expressions and phrases surrounding love. It's extremely important for us to be clear on the terminology. For our purposes, "primitive love" can also be defined as "romantic love" or "falling/being *in* love". I use these terms interchangeably, and often times in tandem for extra clarity. You can also think of primitive love as "chemical love", like a drug---I will explain the reason for this in the next chapter. Basically, all of these terms and expressions describe the feeling we get when we find someone we instinctually want to mate with. Our pulse quickens, and our senses become heightened, making us feel more alive. We often experience nervousness, sweaty palms and dry mouth around this person. We find ourselves thinking about them constantly----often obsessively. This is the feeling the poets write about and the singers sing about. It's a beautiful and powerful thing! I've heard a lot of songs that ask aloud, "Am I in love?/Is this love?" I don't understand why it's so hard to determine. If we have these clear physiological symptoms, **we are in love**. But, one of the major points I want to drive home is: just because we have fallen in love with someone does not mean that we are *meant* to be together.

If we are going to master our fear of falling in love, then we need to deepen our understanding of it, and deepen our understanding of ourselves. In order to do that we must understand the science of love and reach a more in-depth understanding how our brains work. We don't need to get too technical, but we must understand some basic science.

The most primitive part of our brain is referred to as the "reptilian brain" because it is essentially the same brain structure that reptiles, birds, and fish have. The reptilian brain is responsible for life's most basic drives: fight or flight, hunger, and sexual arousal/desire to mate. To understand ourselves and our behaviors, we must grasp that our brains have evolved, and understand why they evolved into their current state. Since these are the primary drives to sustain life, it's logical that they would be extremely primal, and extremely powerful. Problems arise for us when these primal drives go unchecked by the more evolved regions of our brains, our cerebral cortex, or neocortex. By "unchecked", I mean *not consciously examined* to determine whether those drives are justified, or if acting out in response to them is going to suit our overall needs best. If unchecked, these compelling drives can cause us to act out in harmful, destructive ways such as eating junk food, abusing drugs, lashing out in angry words or actions, sexual infidelity and/or unprotected sex—in general, <u>acting in ways that are not aligned with our higher values</u> such as patience, empathy, or love. All of these higher values come from our cerebral cortex (the more evolved parts of our brain). The cerebral cortex can be divided into sub-regions, but for our purposes it's not important to get too specific or too technical.

The point is that the regions contained within the cerebral cortex are responsible for things like empathy, rational thought and logic. Humanity ascended to dominance in the animal kingdom because we learned to team up and work together. We are not the fastest or strongest, but it was our intellect that gave us the upper hand, and it was love that gave us the upper hand. We learned to love each other beyond the scope of our immediate family. It was our ability to love and cooperate that propelled us to dominance in the animal kingdom.

I dedicate an entire chapter later in this book to looking at some of the popular clichés from popular music and contrasting them to my new paradigm, but I want to look at one of those clichés now, because it is so closely tied to the idea of primitive love. Let's consider the phrase 'the head versus the heart." Poetic, yes, but it is crucial to recognize this is a false paradigm. Our emotions do not reside outside of your head. Our heart is a muscle that pumps blood throughout our bodies; it is not the epicenter for our emotions. I think the vast majority of people understand this, but they sometimes lose sight of this truth because of this enduring expression. often hear highly educated people make statements such as, "matters of the heart cannot be comprehended by the brain." But if we want to be technically correct, "matters of the heart" are actually "matters of the primitive brain."

The human brain has three basic regions: the reptilian brain, the limbic system, and the cerebral cortex, but for our purposes, we need only focus on the relationship between the reptilian brain and the cerebral cortex. The eternal battle between these two regions explains the paradigm of "the head versus the heart." The "heart" represents the primitive, selfish and greedy impulses that originate in our reptilian brain. "The head" represents the cerebral cortex and the impulses to be more altruistic; to have empathy, to act responsibly, and fairly.

This inner conflict explains the dual nature of humankind. It explains the enduring power of classic stories like *The Strange Case of Doctor Jekyll and Mr. Hyde*, and the Hermann Hesse novel *Steppenwolf* (in which the main character struggles to figure out and reconcile his dual nature and desires). I think it also helps explain the lasting mythology of werewolves, and the myth of the minotaur from Greek mythology (half man/half bull, completely lacking in self-control or rational thinking).

There's a famous line from Abraham Lincoln's First Inaugural Address where he mentions "the better angels of our nature." The better angels of our nature reside in the more evolved regions of our brain.

Nikos Kazantzakis wrote a beautiful prologue to *The Last Temptation of Christ* which reads, "my principal anguish and the source of all my joys and sorrows from my youth onward has been the incessant, merciless battle between the spirit and the flesh. Within me are the dark immortal forces of the evil one, human and pre-human; within me too other luminous forces, human and pre-human, of God----and my soul is the arena where these two armies have clashed and met." I wish I could tell Kazantzakis that science has solved the mystery of that struggle.

In the Preface to *Fear and Loathing in Las Vegas*, Hunter S. Thompson quotes Samuel Johnson: "HE WHO MAKES A BEAST OF HIMSELF gets rid of the pain of being a man."

Humanity's story is the battle between these regions of the brain that are often in conflict. I think you'll agree that this dynamic also correlates closely to Sigmund Freud's theory that our psyche is divided into three parts: The Id (Selfish/childish impulses), The Super Ego (moral compass/conscience), and the Ego, which ultimately has the final say of choosing what actions we take in response to the struggle between the Id and Super Ego.

Let me go one step further. Think of the classical depiction of the devil in antiquity…the half-man/half-goat figure. Is this not explained by this relationship between our primitive brain and our evolved brain? This is a recurring theme throughout literature and mythology that we can find in various cultures. Consider this Native American parable:

An old Cherokee elder was teaching his grandson about life. He told the boy, "A fight is going on inside me. It is a terrible fight and it is between two wolves. One is evil – he is anger, envy, sorrow, regret, greed, arrogance, self-pity, guilt, resentment, inferiority, lies, false pride, superiority, and ego. The other is good – he is joy, peace, love, hope, serenity, humility, kindness, benevolence, empathy, generosity, truth, compassion, and faith. The same fight is going on inside you – and inside every other person, too."

The grandson thought about it for some time and then asked his grandfather, "Which wolf will win?"

The elder replied, "The one you feed."

It is absolutely crucial that we not only understand the relationship between the reptilian brain to the cerebral cortex, but also decide that, when there is a conflict between these regions, our primitive impulses must capitulate to the rational, logical, evolved regions of our brain. Logic, reason, harmony, and love are the ideals that we must recommit to in a more profound way. The first key to doing this is recognizing that, yes, those primitive, selfish emotions dwell within us all. If we are to conquer these primitive emotions, we can't be in denial about their existence. I think it's also extremely important that we not carry guilt for simply having those primitive, selfish impulses. These impulses are necessary for life, and sometimes it's perfectly fine to act on those primitive feelings. Sometimes having sex, eating a delicious meal, taking our anger out on a punching bag, as examples, are perfectly fine. There is no inner conflict in these cases, and this is where we experience profound joy. When acting on our primal urges does not conflict with our higher values, we can freely indulge in them without guilt.

In the process of coming to grips with our primal urges, it is important that we reexamine our attitude toward *lust*. For too long we've been made to believe that lust is *evil*…something to be ashamed of and feel guilty for. I beg to differ. I think lust is wonderful. It's an amazing feeling. Lust makes us feel incredibly alive, does it not? I do not feel guilty when I am under the spell of lust. Ever. No matter who I am attracted to, or how inappropriate it would be for me to *actually pursue* the object of my lust as a sexual partner, because I understand that **lust is a reflexive, unconscious, natural reaction.** There's no reason to feel guilty for simply *having* attraction to someone. The time to feel guilt would be if we try to pursue someone knowing that it isn't the right thing to do; that someone would get hurt, or that the relationship would be inappropriate for any number of reasons. I see a real problem with the fact that religious teaching has informed us that we should feel ashamed for having lusty thoughts…that we should feel guilty for these perfectly natural and harmless feelings. If we are to deal with these feelings of lust in a healthy way, then it's important that we accept them as natural and harmless. There is no logical reason to feel guilty, and doing so only causes unnecessary and unhealthy psychological turmoil. Feeling guilty and/or beating ourselves up for natural feelings is a recipe for trouble.

These primitive feelings are neither *good* nor *evil*; they are necessary to sustain both individual life, and life on the planet. By allowing ourselves to feel guilty about these natural feelings, we are not only getting our psychology twisted, but I also believe that feeling guilty over a sexual attraction only serves to *heighten* the attraction. "Why should that be the case?" you may ask. I think it's because Nature wants to ensure that we keep reproducing. The more we try to repress these natural feelings, and feel guilty about them, the more intense our sexual desires become. The more society tries to repress these natural and essential desires, the more Nature works on us to overcome them.

The point is, as long as we aren't hurting ourselves or anyone else by acting on those primitive emotions, there is no reason to feel guilty about acting on them. And simply *feeling* those emotions and attractions should never be cause for feeling guilt. By vilifying these perfectly natural impulses, we create a lot of unnecessary psychological anguish, and needless guilt. Those primal, primitive emotions are often the source of deep levels of joy and satisfaction. We mustn't vilify them outright if we want to lead happy, fulfilling lives.

The key here is that these primal emotions must be consciously evaluated and examined before we act on them. We must get in the habit of asking ourselves, "will acting upon these desires be in my best interest? Will acting upon them hurt someone else? I believe that most of us naturally ask these questions in most cases, but I still think we collectively need to work harder to make this a conscious habit in our lives. We will never rise above the destructive emotions and impulses of our primitive brains unless we first acknowledge that those impulses are there. We can't be in denial that they exist, nor should we underestimate how powerful they can be. But each of us must accept that we have the power to override and ignore these destructive impulses with our rational, logical, evolved regions of our brain.

I've said much about the cliché "the head versus the heart" and how it shapes our thinking, and thus hinders our understanding of our nature. One of the major points I make throughout this book is that the phrases that we use <u>shape</u> our concepts, shape our *paradigm* of love, and shape our understanding of ourselves. These false paradigms create confusion and ultimately lead to suffering. I had a lengthy debate with an adult friend of mine about whether the heart is actually the organ responsible for our emotions, since we so often refer to emotions being "matters of the heart." I found it very difficult convincing him that the heart (the organ that pumps blood through our body) had nothing to do with our emotions, that it was a figure of speech. Finally, I asked him to consider the case of someone who has an artificial heart—do they no longer experience emotions? Would someone with a heart transplant now have a different set of emotions and affections? Obviously not.

We must improve the language and the phrases that we use to describe and talk about love and relationships, because how we talk influences how we think about love, and how we act toward each other. By understanding our basic brain structure and function, it becomes clear that our emotions do not come from anywhere but our brain. We begin to realize that we have the ability to consciously overpower, override, and take control of our emotions when they are destructive.

This is our goal: *getting over the fear of love; getting over the lingering pain and disappointment of relationships past; and opening fearlessly to love in the present moment.* I want everyone to love and live fully and fearlessly.

My insights about love are largely based on my own experiences, but they are also based on science and philosophy. When I was a younger man, I was reluctant to learn about the science of falling in love, because I thought that understanding this would somehow dampen or cheapen the magic of the experience. I imagine many of you feel the same way. But if we are going to remove the fear of love, it is vital to understand the science of falling in love; to eliminate the confusion, heartache, disappointment, and ultimately the fear of love. We can't fully give love or enjoy someone else's love if we fear that we might get hurt. With this new understanding of love, we realize it is nothing to fear, and there is no reason to withhold it from anyone. It can never hurt us. The truth is, **no one else has the power to break our heart**. Ultimately, we break our own heart by failing to comprehend the nature of love, and our emotions. We thus set unreasonable expectations of our relationships that reality can never live up to. Let us consider what science says about love...

Chapter 4

The Science of Falling in Love

"Look deep into nature, then you will understand everything better."

—Albert Einstein

When you hear poets and songwriters compare love to a drug, this is actually a pretty astute analogy (if we are talking about primitive love/falling in love). What scientists have observed is that cocaine has basically the same effect on the brain as falling in love. Each lowers the threshold of the pleasure centers of our brain, thus allowing more dopamine and norepinephrine to be released. These are the chemicals that make us feel great. Oxytocin is also released, which makes us want to bond.

Falling in love is powerful, and it is beautiful; but we have to understand that it has a limited shelf life, as does any drug. It's important to understand this and be honest about it. Based on scientific research in recent years using brain scan imaging, the experience of falling/being in love (in other words, the *chemical reaction* of love that creates all the feelings of excitement) typically lasts between 18-30 months. There is a scientific explanation for this. Our brains require novelty in order for dopamine to continue to be released at elevated levels. Our brains *crave* novelty…not just in relationships, but in all aspects of life. Not only do our brains crave novelty, but the opposite is also true; we naturally revolt against repetition and stagnation. Think of the old adage "familiarity breeds contempt." I know it sounds harsh, but there is a lot of truth to it. As a general rule, human beings don't want to listen to the same song, eat the same food, talk to the same person all the time.

This does not mean that two people cannot be extremely happy together for a lifetime, but it is important to understand the science so that we can have reasonable expectations in our relationships. I believe most of the pain and frustration that people experience from relationships is born from having unreasonable expectations that reality can never live up to. This is important, and empowering. Not having a solid grasp of the nature of falling/being in love/primitive love is a big reason for why we get into so much trouble, have so much suffering, disillusionment, cheating, and frustration. We've been blind to the true nature of these emotions, and how our brains behave. Falling in love is real. It is powerful. It is beautiful. But it doesn't last forever. We should not fear it!

Moreover, we need to realize and be honest about the fact that in our lifetime most of us will experience falling in love multiple times. I believe that one or two of those times can be much more intense than the others, but that doesn't mean those people are a better match for us. We shouldn't be surprised, or sad, or resentful of this reality. Being conscious sets us free.

From my own personal experience, I can tell you that the woman I had the most intense feeling of falling in love with was the worst match for me on a personality basis, and the woman that I knew the least about. I fell for her right away because she was incredibly beautiful and sexy in her own right; but more than that, she reminded me of one of my earliest movie star crushes. We dated a few times, but we never had sex, and I never got a chance to really find out who she was, what her ambitions were, and what her values were. After a few dates we had an argument, and she basically stopped talking to me. I knew I had no reason to feel as devastated as I was when it ended. But I *did* feel devastated. Why?

Armed with the "logic" that "when you meet the <u>right</u> person, it's an overwhelming feeling, and you just know that you were meant to be together", I made the mistake of concluding "this is the one God meant for me to be with," and because of that I wove a whole fantasy in my head about the kind of person she was, how wonderful she was, and what a great love story we'd create together. I think this is something we do as human beings; we see a really attractive person, and we unconsciously, automatically, start ascribing positive personality traits to them. For example, I can look at a picture of a beautiful model and I find that I start imagining what kind of person she is, and I find that I assume she has positive traits. I encourage you to give this exercise a try sometime. Sit down and look at faces and start writing down the personality traits that you imagine that person has. See if you don't associate positive attributes to the more attractive faces. I think it's a natural thing to do, and it's important to be aware that we do this.

The mistake that we have made is that we have held up this version of primitive love/romantic love/falling madly in love as the ultimate bond that people should have. More than that, the prevailing wisdom is that when you meet "the one," you fall "madly in love," 'that's the one you're meant to be with," you get married, and live "happily ever after." This conventional wisdom sets us up for heartache and disappointment, and often leads us to attempt romantic partnerships with men and women who are, in fact, terrible partners for us for any number of significant reasons. We can, and most likely will, fall in love with someone who is a terrible partner for us. This has also led many men and women to stay in verbally and physically abusive relationships. They fell deeply in love with someone, and because of the intensity of the attraction made the assumption that they had found the person they were meant to be with; their "soul mate". By and large, we confuse intense "falling in love"/romantic love/primitive love as a sign from God that we are meant to be with that person, and are going to make a great couple. This is a huge mistake.

We must get past the notion that when we fall in love with someone, it means we have found our "soul mate,". The truth is we may have found someone with very few of the qualities that we need to make for a healthy, fulfilling relationship, even for a short term…let alone a lifetime! We must free ourselves of the fantasy that we simply fall in love, and remain in a state of passionate, romantic love for decades. This is the precise reason I didn't enjoy the movie, "The Notebook". To me, that was a totally unrealistic depiction of a couple that have been together for decades and yet somehow still had 'puppy love' for each other. That's not how love works. Sorry. If that's what you want and expect out of love, I sincerely wish you well finding it, but don't be shocked if reality doesn't live up to your expectation.

The fact that romance/being in love doesn't last forever is not a cause for sadness. We can still have great, long-lasting, satisfying relationships. Accepting this truth allows us to appreciate primitive/romantic love while it is present and not take it for granted. It also helps us recognize that love is nothing to fear. This understanding helps us enjoy our relationships more than ever before.

Chapter 5

Evolved/Divine Love Defined

We all love the experience of "falling in love" and we want to experience it without fear. We all want to feel confident pursuing relationships with those we fall in love with. And we can. This is what I want for you. But in order to do this we need to recognize that there is a superior form of love to strive for, to appreciate, and to celebrate. We must define love more clearly, and improve the way we think about, talk about, and show love to one another.

I am excited and hopeful about the kind of relationships and the kind of world we could have if we could put primitive/romantic love in its proper place. **Primitive love is not the ultimate kind of love that human beings can experience and share with one another. We must strive for an evolved form of love**----a love that comes from the more evolved regions of our brain; a love that is not possessive, nor selfish, and doesn't turn to bitterness and hatred when a romantic relationship doesn't work out. This kind of love is not so much an *emotion*, but more of a *thought*. Other names for this kind of love might be "divine love" or "unconditional love." Once we recognize it and appreciate it as we should, I think people around the world will have more satisfying, healthier, longer-lasting relationships. We would recognize that love is not a limited resource, but instead a limitless energy that is meant to be shared with as many people as possible. This is what I have discovered. This works for me, and I'm confident it will work for lots of other people as well.

I love Love! I am open to love without fear. I know that no one can truly hurt me, because I have a clear understanding of what love is and how it works. I believe that a central truth of human existence is that our emotions are most out of control, and frighten us most, when we do not understand what is causing them. We must apply the power of our conscious minds and recognize what is causing our emotions. By having a solid understanding of love, it becomes much easier to expel negative emotions, and remove the fear of love.

Here is my perspective on how we should view and practice love and express and teach our children about love. In contrast to the pop culture concept of love (what I call primitive love), this is my definition of "evolved love"; the "new paradigm" that we should strive for:

Love is the deepest level of *caring* about someone else. It is when we care *so much* about another person, that they *feel like they are part of us*. It's the way that a parent naturally, and automatically loves their child, because they intuitively feel that the child is a part of them or an extension of them.

I'm not a religious man, but I am *spiritual*. I believe that this evolved love, or divine love, or unconditional love is nothing less than recognizing the *deep reality*: **we are all connected**. We are all part of a big system of Life, connected by Love. We all share a common ancestor. Everything that you see and sense around you…every person…every living thing…all non-living things have evolved from stars. All atoms heavier than hydrogen and helium were created in the nuclear fusion of stars. I find this incredibly fascinating and beautiful.

That is my simple definition of love----the "new paradigm" that we should recognize, celebrate, and strive for. Now let us compare and contrast these two versions of love and try to see what they look like in the real world, in the way that we talk about love, and interact with one another.

Chapter 6

The Clichés of Love

There are many clichés in popular music that I have an issue with. I want to analyze and contrast some of these classic clichés to my mature, evolved definition of love. I realize that songwriters seldom set out to write a song with the intention of teaching people how to deal with love and breakups in a thoughtful, level-headed manner. I realize that songs are often born out of a painful, purely emotional reactions to breakups and they're just trying to capture their feelings in words. I think that's the basic drive behind most songs, "write what you feel" hoping that people can relate to that emotion; that this will ultimately help the listener deal with their own pain, and know that someone else understands how they feel…that they are not alone. I get that. But what we are then left with is an abundance of songs that reflect unchecked emotions, and capture nothing of philosophy or logic, nor any attempt to find a constructive, mature way to deal with pain or breakups. Songwriters probably feel that would detract from the emotional impact of a song. Because the vast majority of love songs focus so intensely on the emotion, trying to build an emotional punch…young people and perhaps the public at large grow up to think: "this is how I should deal with a breakup. I should be angry at my ex. I should feel down in the dumps." Or these songs give people the impression that the appropriate way to express fondness for another person is through exaggeration and promises about "happily ever after."

Cliché #1 "I Need You"

We've all been through break ups that made us feel that we could not be happy again, and we've seen friends go through such break ups as well. I know that people oftentimes actually do think this way, and can't convince themselves that they will possibly be happy again...but what ultimately happens? Time passes, and so does the pain. It always does. It may take weeks or months (hopefully not years) but one day, we wake up and realize we are just fine. On some level, we know that the pain will pass, so it is really a kind of insanity to keep telling ourselves that we can't be happy. And all that time feeling depressed, being closed off to love and to life was time squandered. I want to help people get through this phase of grief faster and open to love once more.

Wouldn't it be great to shorten the duration of this insanity? For it is *insane*, right? We know logically and rationally that life goes on, and of course we will be happy again. Part of the problem is that we say it so often that we start to believe it's true. We need to be conscious and careful about our inner dialogue, and with the phrases that we express to each other. The reality is that happiness is an emotion that we can summon at any moment by consciously reflecting on the things that we appreciate, and thinking thoughts of gratitude for all that we have in our life, even if it's only for life itself.

The first step in being able to do this is to simply recognize that we have the power with our conscious mind to summon positive emotions. Break ups can be very emotional, but the sooner we can heal and mend, the sooner we can get back in the game and onto the next relationship. Thus, we will live more fulfilling lives and the lives of those we love will be more fulfilling as well. We leave a lot of untapped potential to love on the fields of life. We must tell ourselves and convince ourselves that we can be happy without that other person. Just think logically; there was a time before you were together when you experienced happiness, right? Remind yourself of that fact.

We can be happy alone. If you struggle with that concept, then you need to work on yourself before you're ready to get involved in a relationship. When someone makes the statement, "I need you", they often say it because they are expected to say that. We've come to believe that this is something you say to someone that you love. We need to change this. By constantly making this statement out loud because it is expected, we inevitably come to believe that this is true. But evolved/divine love has nothing to do with *need*. Somehow we have come to accept that the expression "I need you" is not only healthy, but an actual requirement in a loving relationship. We need to change the way we think and the way we communicate. We are confusing *want* with *need*. Perhaps people think "need" is essentially "want" taken to the highest degree. But I would argue that they are two completely different things, and it's important to distinguish the differences.

Let's think about this phrase: "I need you". Do we *actually* need someone else in order to sustain life? Of course not. What we *actually* need are things like water, air, and food; beyond that, not much else is required to live. And what would we do if someone tried to take those requirements for life away? Tried to take our air; take our water; take our food? Would we manipulate to get those things? Would we lie? Would we go to almost any length to ensure that we have those necessities of life? You see, by saying and thinking "I need you" we create an unhealthy, selfish mindset that actually hinders our ability to love someone else in the way they deserve. More than that, by convincing ourselves that we *need* this other person, it virtually guarantees that we can never treat them right.

I think we also need to ask ourselves: what happens if that person that we need dies? What becomes of us then? What happens if that person that we need decides the relationship is no longer working for them, and they choose to be alone or with someone else? Does that mean that our life is over? That there is nothing worth living for? If you honestly think that your partner is the only reason that you have to live, then you really have to improve your thinking and find other things that give you reason to be happy and appreciative. I hope you can see that telling ourselves that we need someone is not a healthy thing to do, nor is it a factual statement. Our reason for living and your happiness are **not** contingent on any other person. We must learn to recognize this and improve the way we think about our relationships.

Perhaps when people say and think "I need you", it really means "I need you in order to be happy," but this is also untrue, and also creates an unhealthy mindset. We cannot love someone else in a healthy way, in a selfless way by telling ourselves we *need* them in order to be happy; we will always have a selfish desire to keep that person close…. even if they are not happy in the relationship. This is not healthy. This is not in line with my definition of love. We have to find happiness by ourselves, before we can enter a relationship with someone else. The first step to doing this is realizing that we each have the ability to create happiness with our conscious mind; and we can do this by actively practicing joy and gratitude by reflecting on all the reasons that we have to be thankful. We all have reasons to be thankful. Let's make it a daily habit to reflect on our blessings, and be thankful for *all* of our relationships. Evolved love is not about "needing" to be with someone else; it is about "wanting" to be with someone else. *Wanting* is more of an honest concept, and is a much healthier way to think about the affection we have for another person, and our desire to be with them.

In my own relationships in recent years, I have made it a point to be very clear with the women I have been involved with, "I am in love with you, but more importantly, I *love* you. I respect and appreciate you. I think you are awesome! ...and I love being with you. But what's more important to me than my selfish desire to be with you, is your happiness. If the day comes when you are not happy with me, or you realize that I am not a good fit for you, I will let you go. And I will love and respect you no less. I will still care deeply for you." These aren't just words. This is a true expression of how I feel. It's a beautiful thing to love someone this way, and have them love you the same way in return.

Cliché #2 "I can't live without you."

The sister of "I need you" is "I can't live without you." These are phrases that a person would say to manipulate the other person to stay. The point I'm trying to make is that the phrases we use to talk about love and relationships greatly influence the way we think about our relationships. And often create problems in our relationships. If you keep saying that you *can't live without someone*, you actually start to believe that it is true. Deep down, we all know that we can go on after a breakup and be happy again. Let's acknowledge that now, and stop telling ourselves these misleading and destructive thoughts. If you are going to give love to someone in a healthy way, then you must remove the fear that someday that might leave you, cheat on you, and devastate you. Recognize that yes, they may leave, cheat on you...they might even die...but they cannot devastate you. You must convince yourself and tell yourself that no matter what happens, you are going to have plenty of other reasons to go on in life and be happy. Remind yourself of this fact, "no matter what happens, I am going to be fine." You have the power to choose how you will react. Own it.

Love is an emotion but it is also a thought, and a verb. And the opposite of the verb *to love*, is <u>to use</u>. You would never *use* someone that you loved and cared deeply about. Because that is not allowing them freedom. And that is not respecting them. Think about how many times you have heard this line in pop music, or perhaps in your personal life, "you were just using me." The harsh truth is if our relationship was based solely on primitive/romantic love, then we basically were using each other, although we didn't think of it that way. One of the reasons we get into relationships to feel better. It's the same reason people use drugs: to feel better. I think most of us were unaware that our motives were selfish. We didn't realize that, indeed, were using our partner. We've largely been raised to believe that primitive/romantic love is enough to carry us through relationships, that if the feelings were strong enough they would last a lifetime. My point is, primitive/romantic love is not enough to base a serious relationship upon. Falling in love is only the first part of a larger puzzle. We must also develop a deeper, more evolved and conscious love; the unconditional love, which is the deepest level of caring about someone else. This can only happen over time, by getting to know each other's soul. When we love someone this way, no matter how strong the romantic feelings that we have and how much we want to be with this person... ultimately we put their happiness above our own selfish desires. We want to be with this person, but only so long as they are truly happy and satisfied being with us.

If we do not take the time to develop evolved love in our relationships, and recognize it as the superior form of love then we don't have much of a relationship at all. Part of our collective problem stems from the fact that we hold this romantic, primitive, "falling in love," "love at first sight" as the be-all and end-all of human existence….as the ultimate bond that two people can have; but it's not. We can fall in love with someone we hardly know, but we can't *fully love* someone that you hardly know. This concept of love at first sight is akin to infatuation. Once again, just because we fell in love, no matter how intoxicating and overwhelming it might feel, it doesn't *guarantee* that we are going to be a good match for each other for any amount of time, let alone a lifetime. We can, and most likely will fall in love with people who would be a terrible match for us. I'll talk about this in more detail a bit later, but I want to introduce you to this concept now.

Telling ourselves that we literally can't go on without someone else is also leads to an unhealthy obsession, that often turns into bitter jealousy after a breakup. Consider the song "Every Breath You Take" by The Police. The songwriter Sting has said that he was inspired by reading *Frankenstein*, specifically by how the monster obsessed over Dr. Frankenstein, his creator. It reminded him of the obsessive and negative feelings that he was dealing with after the end of his first marriage. The public at large heard the song and thought it was a lovely romantic song. A lot of people have been married to that song. Does that not indicate that the way we talk and think about love as a society needs improvement?

Love has *nothing to do with possession*. Love has everything to do with allowing the other person freedom. Love means wanting the other person to be happy, and freedom is a prerequisite to happiness.

I can honestly tell you that if my partner wanted to be with someone else I would not lose a night's sleep over it, because I am rational and I understand love. If my partner no longer wants to be with me, I accept it without any hard feelings. It doesn't diminish the respect, admiration, and love that I have for them. Why should it? Unlike so many others, I also don't take it as a blow to my self-esteem. I have high self-esteem, meaning I like myself. I'm proud of the person I have become and am striving to become, but I know full-well that I am not the right guy for every woman. Why would it be a shock if a woman realizes I'm not the right fit for her? Or that I am no longer the right fit for her? How could I be upset with her? I'm still happy even if I am by myself. One more thing I want to stress about my views on relationships that I hope more people will understand: **I love myself enough that I only want someone to be with me *if they want to be with me.*** I hope this makes sense. I hope that more people will start to think this way, because if they thought about relationships this way, there would be much less angst, sadness, and bitterness after a breakup. This mindset is a big reason why I am able to give love fearlessly, and why I am still able to care deeply for anyone I have ever been involved with. **If you love yourself, you would never ask someone to stay with you out of guilt or out of an obligation; you want someone to be with you who truly enjoys being with you and is deeply satisfied with the relationship.**

I think it's also important to be mature and accept the reality that our partner, at some point, will have a desire to be with someone else. I'm not talking about sex (yet), I'm simply talking about spending quality bonding time, and having meaningful conversations with other people...sometimes even people of the opposite sex! I have no idea what percentage of adults have a hard time with this reality, but I've heard about it often enough from friends and in my own relationships that I recognize it's a real issue that we must mature on. No matter how wonderful we are, and how much fun we have with our partner, they will need other people to talk to and spend time with feel happy and fulfilled. If we care about our partner and want them to be happy, then we need to allow them the freedom to spend time with others that make them happy, even if those others are of the opposite sex. There is no argument about this. If we can't grant our partner that freedom and trust then either we do not fully love our partner, or we have self-esteem issues that we must work on. Of course, our partner should grant us the same freedom. As always, it is a two-way street.

Now let's talk honestly about sex. We have to be honest about this too. No matter how attractive and sexy we are, our partner is still going to be attracted to other people. Let's not lie to ourselves or each other any longer. Let's mature on this. One point I want to make is: the fact that we may be sexually attracted to other people is not a reflection of how attracted we are to our partner. We can care deeply for our partner, and be very much in love with our partner, and still be extremely attracted to other people that come along. As I pointed out earlier, "falling in love" happens automatically, reflexively…within a fraction of a second. Falling in love does not require conscious thought, therefor it's nothing to feel guilty about, or confused over. Just because we fall in love with someone else does not mean we're not in love with our partner, or that we are with the wrong person. For myself, when I am in love with my partner and our relationship is working, even though I might be attracted to someone else, there is no *real* desire to be with anyone else. There is no temptation to stray. Should I meet someone new that I am extremely attracted to it doesn't rock my world and make me question the relationship I am in. I don't feel guilty about the attraction. I anticipate it will happen so it makes it very easy to dismiss and not get caught up in it. **When I am in love, and the relationship is working, I don't want to do anything to dampen or diminish the feelings that I have for my partner.** I know that it's rare to have everything I am looking for in a relationship, and I want to invest in and nurture it; not through it away or tarnish it by pursuing some random infatuation. I don't view "falling in love" as the ultimate thing in life. I no longer make the mistake of thinking that falling in love with someone means that I am *supposed* to be with them, or that we will be happy together.

Love is not about *needing* someone else; it's about *wanting*. Our inner dialogue should say "I want to be with my partner", rather than "I need to be with my partner." Our dialogue with each other needs to change also. We need to stop saying to each other, "I need you." We need to put an end to this. It causes pain, confusion, and fear of love. It's this line of thinking that convinces people to stay in abusive relationships.

When we see men and women stay in abusive relationships, I think it largely because of the flawed logic of thinking "I need you." So many have bought into this romantic notion that they literally can't go on without the other person. They honestly believe that there's just one person in the whole world they are "meant for." It gives rise to the idea that if you *truly* love someone, you would stay with them *no matter what*. Again, I point to pop culture for reinforcing this notion. This leads to several real-world problems.

For one thing, this faulty logic leads people to think that it is proper and noble to stay in abusive relationships. I think many of us wonder why someone would choose to stay in an abusive relationship. I believe it is explained by the popular idea that <u>loving</u>

someone means you stay with them **no matter what**. We must liberate ourselves from this kind of thinking. I think part of the reason that so many of us stay in these relationships is because we do not have healthy self-esteem----we do not love themselves. I will explain in my own way what it means to "love yourself" in Chapter 7, and why it's so crucial to achieve before getting into any relationship.

Consider this: part of the marriage vow is to remain together "for better or worse." I have a huge problem with this vow. Am I missing something, or does this vow imply that there are no valid reasons to split up after a marriage? Of course there are valid reasons to split up, and abuse should be right at the top of the list. How bad must "worse" be before a person can honorably separate from an abusive spouse? In my opinion, if your relationship is making you unhappy or is not satisfying, that is cause enough to end a relationship. We all deserve to be happy. Life is short. At the point of physical or verbal abuse, there should be no question and no hesitation: you should separate. No guilt or shame; no second-guessing…get out.

Let me make an important point here: I'm not saying that we need to stop loving and caring about that person we separate from. I'm simply saying we should not live with this person and continue to put up with the abuse. No one deserves that treatment. Beyond that, if we stay in abusive relationships then we are not helping our partner recognize that they need to change their behavior. What our partner needs from us in this case is tough love. One of the key characteristics I require in a working relationship is that each of us **challenge each other to grow**, to get better, to improve. In chapter 10 I list the essential characteristics that should be found in any healthy, working relationship, but one of them is simply challenging each other to grow. In other words, calling each other out on our actions and habits that need improvement. When we are not living up to our highest selves, I think partners ought to challenge each other to be better, and to be people of integrity and kindness. When couples address these things doesn't have to be an argument; it should be a level-headed, nonjudgmental discussion about what you could each be doing to become better partners and better people in general. It has to be done lovingly, but it has to be done. Partners owe that to each other. If our partner is abusive, and we stay in that relationship then we are not giving them the clear message that they **need to change**; for their own sake as much as our own. They must work to defeat whatever demons they have that are producing the abusive behavior, and they need to do that on their own.

Cliché #3 Passing "The Test of Time"

Here's another cliché from pop music that I believe needs to be retired. How many songs have you heard that reference the idea that love must "pass the test of time"? The implication being that *if love is real, it will last forever*, and if the relationship doesn't last forever, then it obviously means the love wasn't real or special.

Here is what I think: if the "love" being referred to is primitive love/romantic love, then **time has nothing to do with whether it was** *real* **or not**. In other words, whether the feeling lasts for eight days or eight years…it is real. And we must recognize that primitive love is not designed to last. It is a chemical, emotional reaction that naturally fades over time. If we expect the romance to last forever we are setting ourselves up for disappointment and confusion, and, tragically we won't appreciate the time we did have in those relationships, and the love we shared.

On the other hand, if we are talking about evolved love, unconditional love, the love that you have for friends and family that I'm outlining…then **that is a love that may very well last**, that is something we can reasonably promise into the future. In much the same way that a parent will always love their child; no matter what differences, or intense arguments and fights they have with their children, they still love them…even if they can't always express it. Virtually all parents will always want the best for their children. It is evolved love that has lasting power.

I expect a lot of people will have a hard time accepting that being "in love" doesn't last for years and years, but it is so important to understand for many reasons. Understanding that the feeling will not last, **we now appreciate every day and every moment that we have love**. It heightens our sense of love and we are much more inclined not to take our partner for granted. We don't take our time spent together for granted. We are now predisposed to drink up and savor the experience. We have heard the advice, "live each day like it is your last." That makes sense right? Well, I would advise, "love each day like it is your last." When we love this way, we put effort into our relationship and fully experience it. We are much more inclined spend our time with our partner enjoying *meaningful* conversations and experiences. We appreciate each other more. And should the day come when the romance is no longer there…there is no shock or sadness or thinking that the love wasn't real or was somehow a waste of time. No one knows how long the romance with last, so appreciate each day.

I remember my own disappointment when my first girlfriend broke up with me, I remember having the thought that all the time we spent together was a *waste* because it didn't last. I thought we were building a relationship that would just get stronger and stronger and last a lifetime. That was my hope for the relationship, and that was my *expectation*. It was my **expectation that was the problem**. When you see love as I now do, whatever time you have together is never a waste of time. Life is better when we are spending time with someone, or others that we care about. In the same way that we enjoy a roller coaster ride at the amusement park, should we think of it as a waste of time when the ride comes to an end? Of course not. If we had great experiences with our partner and learned from each other, then it was time well spent! It was anything but a waste. We should try to fill our days with as much love as we can. And learn to appreciate those moments and cherish the memories.

Let me give you another thought experiment: imagine that you are single and you are on a two-week vacation to a foreign country. You don't anticipate that you will ever make it back to visit this country again in the future. The question is: Would you be open to falling deeply in love with someone during that two-week vacation? Knowing that you would have to say goodbye at the end of the trip, and likely never see them again?

Would you protect your heart and be closed off to love? Would you open your heart knowing that you would have to say goodbye so soon? What I want to suggest to you is that you absolutely should be open to loving 100%, even though you have to say goodbye. **Fill your days with love**. Appreciate the time you have together, knowing that it's not going to last forever anyway. There is no one person on this planet who is going to make your life happy or complete you. The idea of the "one who got away" is bogus. It wasn't meant to be. Turn the page. I always cringe when I hear a romantic love song about someone pining away for a lover whom it is now impossible to be with...so they spend their days being lonely and sad. I think that's an awful message and gives people the idea that if they can't be with someone in particular, they should rot away and be miserable.

We have to realize that we could die tomorrow, or a week from now. Would we rather spend that time with someone, getting to know and care about them, sharing love...or, being alone and sad? Life is meant to be a shared experience. An intrinsic part of life is connecting to others. We are social creatures. We cannot connect if we are not open. We cannot be open if we are afraid. Fear keeps us closed and alone. I'm not even talking about sex here, I'm just talking about spending time with and bonding with someone. There are lots of wonderful people out there who are going to teach us different things and push us to grow in new ways. Most of us *need* multiple loving relationships in our lives to feel happy and fulfilled. I flatly reject the prevailing concept I can be deeply happy with one person that I love above all others. **Love only goes so deep.** I cannot love my partner any *deeper* than I love my family or my closest friends. They all feel like part of me, and it goes no deeper than that. You might ask, "Isn't it a different love that you have for your partner or spouse?" Yes, it is different. It's a different *flavor* of love. A "'spicier" flavor perhaps, but it is not *deeper,* or stronger than the love I have for friends and family.

Cliché #4 "The Way You Make Me Feel"

Here's another indication that someone's feelings equate to primitive love. How many times have you heard it in pop music, or perhaps thought it to yourself when you fall in love, "I love you because of the way you *make me feel*," or "you make me feel so alive"?

Again, it is wonderful to feel this way, and it is meant to be enjoyed and appreciated. However, having these feelings doesn't mean this person is going to have all the other qualities that we require to have a successful, long-term or even short-term relationship. We can and will fall in love with people that are not a good match for us. Knowing this, we should now feel motivated to pursue those people and find out if we are compatible!

There is no logical reason to hold back. We should pursue those relationships with curiosity and optimism. But we mustn't be surprised or disappointed if we don't find all the qualities that we are looking for in a partner...or that they didn't find the qualities they were looking for in us. The fact that it doesn't work out doesn't mean there is anything *wrong* with either of us; we're simply not a good match. Life goes on. It doesn't mean the time we spent together was wasted. If we had fun together, and learned from the experience, then that time well spent. I think it's more fulfilling and more fun to spend time with someone else than spending that time being alone. Don't you? Life is all about connecting to others. Let's get out there and find someone to spend time with!

At the same time, we must learn to recognize when our inner dialogue say that we love someone because they excite us, we love them because of "the way you make us feel", because they make us feel so alive... it's primitive love that we are experiencing. Primitive love is not enough to sustain a healthy relationship. We experience these feelings without even knowing anything about a person. Experiencing these feelings is not an indication that we are necessarily going to be a good match with the person who makes us feel this way. How many stories have you heard about couples that got married after one week because they were so head over heels in love with each other? The "whirlwind romance"? Big mistake! I understand why some couples do this. It is because they have been raised with the guidance that "when you meet the right person, it's such an overwhelming feeling and you just know that that is the one you are meant to be with". They lacked a real understanding about the nature of falling in love. You can both fall madly in love with each other, and yet be a terrible match for any amount of time, let alone a lifetime.

Because I understand this, I have no fear of pursuing someone that I am attracted to. I have no fear of falling head over heels in love. I fully comprehend that in all likelihood we're not both going to have all the qualities that we each require to make a fun and healthy relationship. My expectations are realistic. When I fall in love I am *optimistic* about finding all those other qualities I need, but should I not find all those qualities it's not shocking nor disappointing to me. There is no logical reason to feel disappointed. I simply accept that we are not a good match for each other and I move on. This is one of the reasons that I can plunge into relationships fearlessly. Because I realize how hard it is to find all of the qualities that I'm looking for in a partner, I know I need to be *actively looking*. It motivates me to get me in the game; to flirt with women that I am attracted to, and pursue relationships with them. I don't expect to find a great match just by pure luck. I know that I need to be looking and flirting. Beyond that, when I find those qualities in someone, I cherish and appreciate it! That's a relationship that I'm going to put effort into because I want it to last as long as possible. Here is one of the great benefits to my approach to relationships that you may not have thought of: when we find a great partner, and there is no promise of staying together, it *motivates us to put effort into the relationship.* If we are having a great time and want to keep spending time with that person, then you'd better put effort into the relationship to keep them interested.

I want to introduce an analogy that I think will help you approach falling in love and starting new relationships with a healthy attitude...so that you do enjoy the experience *without* the fear of disappointment or heartbreak. I encourage you to approach your relationships with the same mindset with which you would approach a roller coaster ride (unless roller coasters terrify you, in which case, this of another kind of fun ride that doesn't terrify you!). In the first chapter I said falling in love can feel scary, like being on a wild car ride with no brakes. This is a similar analogy, but the difference is, with a roller coaster, you know you that the ride is going to be safe. You are not going to lose an arm or a leg, and your cart is not going to fly off the track! You should have the intention that the experience is going to be fun. You don't know where it is going or how long it's going to last, but if you are going to enjoy the ride you can't be afraid of getting hurt or dying. You have to know at the outset that there are going to be ups and downs and thrills, but you will end up safe on the ground afterward. And you will have been enriched by the experience.

Also, realize that this ride is not going to last forever. It cannot. Romantic love/being in love does not last forever. By getting on the ride and expecting it to last forever, you are setting yourself up for disappointment. Furthermore, when the ride is over, don't think of it as a waste of time or a failure. If the two of you had great times together, if you learned from each other, and helped each other grow...that is a success! That is time well spent. That is reason to be deeply appreciative; both for the experience and for the person with whom you shared the experience. The element of time is not a factor in my equation for success. At the point in time when your relationship is no longer fun or no longer working for any reason, accept it. It is what it is. If you both think it's something you can fix, and willing to work on it, but all means try. If not, accept it, but also *appreciate* the experience that you shared together! One of the saddest things that I see after couples break up is that they so often view the time spent together as a waste, and tend to harbor ill feelings toward each other. If you had fun together, grew together, learned from each other, laughed together, how can you consider that a waste? Just because two people do not work out as a romantic couple for an entire lifetime, does that mean they should stop caring about each other? I don't think so.

Cliché #5 "The key to your heart"

It always bothers me when I hear a song imply that *someone else* has "the key to our heart." I think this is completely backwards. We each have the key to our own heart. And the lock around our heart has a name. The name is FEAR. If we are ever to love fully and zealously, then we must remove that lock ourselves, by mastering our fear. No one else can do it for you. My deepest desire is to help you remove that lock; not just for your individual happiness, but for the sake of the world. The world needs more love.

Sometimes we've heard songs express something along the lines of, "I'll open my heart to you if you promise not to hurt me." That kind of thinking is not going to cut it, for several reasons. This statement screams, "I am afraid you are going to hurt me!". We should all mature to the point that we can open our hearts fully and fearlessly without any demands or requests from others. "If you promise not to hurt me" can be translated as, "If you promise not to *leave* me". No one can promise that any relationship will last any amount of time. We have to give the relationship a try…fearlessly, and see how it works out. We have to know that it probably not going to be the relationship that lasts the rest of our lives, and know that we are going to be fine regardless. We remove the fear by being aware and logical. This is what this whole book is about. Once you accept this premise, all the other pieces fall into place as logical extensions, and a whole new, less scary, more beautiful, and more exciting view of love begins to come into view.

If you accept the premise that romantic love can still be real and wonderful *and yet* finite…it no longer makes sense to invest so much of your ego and self-worth into making sure that the relationship lasts a lifetime. Let's think rationally. How many relationships have we tried in the past? How many relationships have we tried that didn't work out for even a year? Most people are going to try several, oftentimes many relationships before finding a great match. From a mathematical/statistical standpoint, let's just be wise enough to realize that our current relationship, or the next relationship we're in {no matter how strong our feelings are), the odds are that the relationships is not going to be last for the rest of our life. Knowing this at the start of the relationship also helps remove the fear of trying. Don't be shocked or surprised if they day comes when you are no longer truly happy together. Don't get me wrong, if that's what you are hoping for I wish you all the success in the world; I hope you find it. But it's important that you know that the odds are against it. Love at first sight is real, but let's recognize the kind of love that it is. It is primitive love; largely the result of lust and infatuation. It's just like a drug. It's powerful. But it is a selfish love. Once we recognize this kind of love for what it is we can now enjoy it as we enjoy a beautiful sunset or a blooming flower. We must appreciate while it lasts knowing that it isn't meant to last forever.

Cliché #6 "I'll never let you go"

We hear this line constantly in pop music. It's not a healthy attitude to have toward your partner. What if our partner *wants* to go? What if our partner isn't happy in the relationship? I know that songwriters use this expression, and partners say this expression because we have come to accept that it as a romantic thing to say, and I agree---it is romantic/primitive in the negative sense. As I have pointed out, possessiveness and neediness are the feelings that come with romantic/primitive love. However, if we truly love someone in a healthy, evolved way; if we care deeply for our partner and prioritize *their* happiness, we *must* let them go. Simply put, **the ultimate way to demonstrate evolved/unconditional love for another person is to let them go, and still care just as deeply about them**. No guilt. No hard feelings. It's the same way that a parent must ultimately let their child leave the house and when they have grown. No matter how much a parent wants their child to remain close to home, they realize that someday their child will leave so that they can live their own life. Here we see the stark contrast between these two concepts of love: primitive love is essentially loving someone with a closed fist/holding on; evolved love is loving with an open hand/being able to let go. Loving with an open hand is what we should be striving for.

Cliché #7 "All my love is for you"

We've heard variations of this idea over the decades. I realize it sounds romantic, but like the other cliché's, if we think about the implications of such a statement it's actually a misleading statement, and leads us to believe that love is somehow a *finite resource.* Love is the most abundant resource in the Universe; it is infinite. When you understand the nature of love, you would never think nor say "all of my love". Certainly not that all of your love was for just one person. When we understand love, we recognize that we can feel it, give it, show it fully over and over again to our family, friends, and partner. Opening ourselves to loving more and more people does not diminish the love we feel for any one individual. We must stop thinking in terms of love being a limited, finite resource that should only be shared with a select few. Naturally there will be those closest to us that we will choose to take a more active role in supporting and spending time with, but we must consciously adapt a mindset that says we should try to care deeply for as many people as possible. In doing this we feel more connected, happier, and as more and more people do the same we can lift up the world.

Cliché #8 "You're my world"

Let's reflect on some other pop music love song clichés that we must re-examine; lines such as "baby you are my world"; "you are my everything"; "without you I am nothing." Listening to pop music on the radio over the decades makes me wonder if these songs are written by adults, or school children. I hear a real lack of emotional maturity. Messages like these that we hear so often in our culture do real harm by stoking the flames of people's misery, adding to the confusion, and giving people a sense of validity for their overly emotional response to love and break ups. I think it is a shame because these songwriters and singers could be spreading messages that are helpful instead, as was heard in much of the popular music of the 1960's. I think we need a cultural revolution like that again. "You are my world". "If you ever leave me I don't know what I would do". "Your love is all I need". "You're my reason for breathing". "Please promise me you'll never leave me." And on and on. It's a juvenile mentality and it's not healthy. These are the thoughts of someone with serious self-esteem issues and co-dependency issues. Each statement is, in fact, an attempt at manipulation, and should never be thought and certainly not shared aloud with someone that you care for.

Neediness of this sort is completely unattractive. Plus, it's just bad philosophy. It's unsound philosophy. It's not healthy to think this way. If this sentiment was true, what would we do if our loved one died the next day? Or simply decided to leave? What if our partner found someone else that they would rather be with? Thinking like this, of course we would feel devastated, perhaps even suicidal. But the reality is:. **we would still have plenty of reasons to live and be happy**. We would still have friends and family and a purpose to be in the world. If you don't see this, then you have something to work on. One person should never be the difference between happiness and despair. One person cannot "make or break" us.

What happened to the wisdom of, "Don't put all your eggs in one basket?" It's good investment advice, and it's good advice for life. It's foolish to put "all your eggs into one basket", because if that basket goes…you're screwed! If that one thing disappears, you're not going to recognize and appreciate all the other blessings that you have in your life. It's not a healthy mindset or philosophy to mentally invest your happiness and fulfillment in one relationship. Yet that is exactly what so many people do. They tell themselves that the relationship with their partner will make or break their life and their happiness. This is not true, and it's not a healthy way to think.

So here is another case where I think we **need to change the way we think about and express love**. The problem is that when we hear these expressions attributable to primitive/selfish love so often in popular culture, that we start to think those thoughts and express those thoughts to one another. Thus we develop an unhealthy perception of love and break ups. Our culture has prioritized romantic/selfish/primitive love, and it has birthed a society of co-dependent adults who are confused and afraid to love, and as a result we unnecessarily experience extreme emotional pain from breakups. We may not go to the extreme of killing ourselves when a relationship ends, but we still tend to blow the event out of proportion and suffer needless pain. People actually believe that "their world" and their life is over. They think that's how it's *supposed* to feel when the one you love no longer loves you.

It doesn't have to be this way. Romantic love is wonderful. It makes us feel great. It's fun. But it's not going to give you "heaven," or long term happiness and fulfillment, nor make your life complete. All those things are found in the other kind of love—the evolved love, the divine love, the unconditional love that you have for friends and family, and hopefully your partner as well. That's the love that we should revere, strive for, cultivate and share with as many people as possible. Of course it is natural to have a deeper love for the people we are closest to you, but it is still possible to love the world.

Cliché #9 "What went wrong? We were so in love..."

How often have you heard some variation of this in pop music? This is another pop music trope that I want to put under the microscope. I want it known, nothing went wrong! Romance fades. That's the way romance/being in love works.

Romantic/primitive/being "in love" does not last forever. Understanding this, we can now have reasonable expectations, and realize there is nothing to fear from falling in love. Take that ride with abandon! Life is short, live it. Love. Fearlessly. Think of all the tabloid headlines: "They seemed so in love/ they were so perfect together/ they looked so good together…what went wrong?!" Time after time, the question of "what went wrong?" "It didn't last so clearly there must be something wrong with us, right? That must be why didn't last."

Nature does not need us to be happy together for the rest of our lives. Nature/the universe/God gives us primitive love/falling in love to ensure that we find mates, reproduce, and stay together long enough to ensure healthy, viable offspring that live to adulthood. Beyond that, staying together for the rest of our lives is irrelevant in the eyes of Nature.

Cliché #10 "Love at First Sight"

Let's examine the phenomenon of "love at first sight." I think we will find that people are split in their opinions about whether or not "love at first sight" is a real phenomenon. Many people would argue that this is real, and many would also argue that it's not real. I know I used to argue about it when I was younger. And this is another indication that we have two differing concepts of what it means *to love*. It's the difference of "falling/being in love" as opposed to "loving/growing to love," as I have said repeatedly.

Love at first sight is real if you're talking about falling in love/primitive love. Recent research proves that people "fall in love" within a fraction of a second. In other words, all of the chemical and biological reactions happen instantaneously. So let's be clear: "Love at first sight" is real and it is powerful. It's intoxicating (as is any other drug), but it is *primitive*, and is not designed to last for years and years. Don't get me wrong, I'm a *huge* fan of this feeling. I love the sensation of falling in love, but *I appreciate it for what it is*. I don't fool myself into thinking "here's the one I meant for! I've finally found the love of a lifetime!"… no matter how strong the feeling is. Rest assured though, I am going to pursue that woman I am attracted to (if it's appropriate), because I want to find out if she has all the other qualities I am looking for. I want to find out if we are a good match. If both parties are feeling the same attraction, and they recognize the feeling for what it is (infatuation, lust, and temporary), then they can approach the relationship fearlessly, and have a fantastic time together!

This is what I want for everyone. Recognize and appreciate those feelings because they're too rare. Appreciate those feelings while they live and have a great time. Don't take them for granted. The problems stem from our fantasy that romantic love can bring a lifetime of happiness and fulfillment…this just sets us up for disappointment, disillusion, and heartbreak. It's like getting on a roller coaster expecting that it's going to last the rest of our life. When it inevitably ends, we feel disappointed, rather than appreciating the great experience we've just had.

Chapter 7

Love Yourself

If we are going to remove the fear of falling in love, then we must remove the fear of heartbreak. We must find a way to remove the pain and disappointment when relationships do not work out. In order to do this, we must first learn to love ourselves. I know you have heard this before, but I still want to cover this concept because I haven't heard anyone explain what it means to "love yourself" the same way I do. We need to have a clear definition of what the phrase means, and understand what our internal dialogue should sound like when we actually do love ourselves. In simplest terms, **loving yourself = liking yourself**. When we love ourselves it means that we are proud of the kind of person that we are, and proud of the person that we are working to become. Love of oneself is developed through the daily struggles to become better; to develop the same qualities in *our* character that we value in others; such as patience, empathy, courage, honesty, integrity, and tolerance. We have a sense of satisfaction for the work we have done in order to learn, grow, achieve and help others. We honestly believe that anyone that we might get into a relationship with would be better off for the experience. That does not mean we see ourselves as *perfect,* of course; but we believe that we are a good, and constantly strive to become better. **When we love ourselves, we have an internal dialogue that tells us that we are *worthy* of being loved by an amazing person, and that we deserve to be happy.**

If we truly love ourselves the way we should, we would realize that there is no one who is "out of our league." I've heard it said that it's a fine line between self-confidence and arrogance. It may be a fine line, but it is a *clear* line: self-confidence means *feeling equal to* anyone and everyone; arrogance is *feeling superior to* anyone and/or everyone. It should be easy to recognize whether we have a healthy self-confidence or are arrogant by examining our inner dialogue; and it should be easy to identify in someone else by their words and behaviors.

When I talk about self-confidence and feeling worthy of love, one quality I am not factoring in is physical attractiveness. For one thing, *"beauty" is a completely subjective concept.* In the eyes of our Creator **no one is *more beautiful* than anyone else.** I think it's worth pointing this out and reminding ourselves of this fact. The other reason I don't include physical attractiveness, or height…is because these are qualities that we have not *earned.* We must realize that a healthy self-esteem should be built on having solid character, having integrity, being someone who struggles to become a better person and do more to help others. Ultimately, loving ourselves means reaching a point in our maturity when *we don't need anyone else* to improve our self-esteem, or *validate* us as men and women.

If we enter romantic relationships before we have learned to love ourselves, then we come into those relationships feeling *needy*…which leads to a few problems. For one thing we will likely make poor decisions in choosing a partner, because we won't be as selective, and we tend to rush into relationships with people that are not suitable matches. Secondly, neediness is not an attractive quality when we are trying to attract a partner. Neediness is a big turn off for most people, unless they are looking for someone to take advantage of. The third problem is that, if by change we get lucky and find an excellent partner, that neediness and lack of self-esteem will translate to a lack of trust in our partner. Trust in mandatory in any healthy relationship. Without trust, our relationships are on borrowed time.

So let us be clear: neediness has no place in a healthy relationship. It's neither healthy nor attractive. Neediness is the saboteur of healthy relationships. A healthy love is not about *need* but about *want*. Our inner dialogue should reflect this. And here, once again, I believe we see the battle between the selfish reptilian brain and the evolved cerebral cortex. Our primitive brain thinks "need"/our evolved brain thinks "want."

Loving oneself means coming to the conclusion that we are worthy and deserving of a wonderful partner, and a deeply satisfying, fun, supportive, amazing relationship. The truth is we are all worthy and deserving of just that. Believe it, and strive to find that great partner and create that great relationship! And enjoy the journey. Most likely we will have to try many relationships before finding a great match. Knowing this at the outset, it doesn't make sense to get discouraged if we have to keep trying. In the process we are likely to meet lots of wonderful people, and we will grow and learn from each relationship. Have the intention that whatever the outcome of the romance, that you will still appreciate and care about each other should it not work out.

If a person hasn't yet learned to love oneself; that's ok. But work must be done to build self-esteem before we can love fearlessly and have a healthy relationship. Put another way, in order to have a healthy relationship with someone else, we must first have a healthy relationship with ourselves. It will be harder for some to reach the stage of loving/liking yourself, believing that we are worthy…but we *must* get there if we are ever going to fully give and experience loving someone else. I strongly suggest spending some time being single and working on personal development. Let us face ourselves in the mirror and honestly ask: "What are the areas of my character that I need to work on?" The reality is that all of us should be constantly working on self-improvement. We will never completely fix all of the issues that we have, but it's the effort to improve that matters. It is a profoundly satisfying feeling to struggle and to make progress in life. I think this is why so many of us enjoy exercising and lifting weights. From struggle comes progress, and we instinctively find satisfaction and experience improved self-esteem in the process. You are as worthy of love as anyone else in this world. Every event that had to transpire in the history of the Universe for you to be here right now…has transpired. You are no accident. You are special and deserving of amazing relationships.

Part of the problem is that so many men and women have come to believe that their self-worth is determined by a) whether we have a partner/spouse, and b) who our partner is; how "successful" or "attractive" they are (I use quotes because, again, those terms are subjective. When I was younger, I used to think like this too. On some level of consciousness I thought that having an extremely attractive girlfriend or wife would not only feel better about myself, but also earn me higher esteem from my peers…as if that would be some great accomplishment. It's embarrassing now to admit that I actually used to think this way. But I am admitting it because I believe this is common thinking for both men and women. We need to recognize that this kind of thinking is immature and unhealthy.

We must individually and collectively realize that our partner does not define us. Our partner, or lack thereof, is not a reflection on us as people. Realizing that our partner does not define us, we also recognize that we should not be devastated should our partner leave.

As mature adults with a healthy self-esteem, we need to recognize that breakups should not affect our self-esteem. We are the same person with or without a partner. In reality, the attractiveness of our partner has <u>nothing</u> to do with our value as a human being. Even if we are dating a wealthy celebrity model or the "sexiest man or woman alive" we must be aware of the fact that, just because our partner enjoys our company or finds us attractive, it does not validate us as a person to even the slightest degree. We are who you are, with all the same strengths and weaknesses, regardless of who our partner is or is not. For the mature men and women who understand this, and have learned to love themselves, their self-esteem is neither inflated not deflated by their partner. They understand that they will be fine either way.

We must mature and recognize that not everyone is going to share our values and aspirations in life, and therefore not everyone is going to be a good match for us. There's nothing wrong with that. Everyone is entitled to their own values, and free to look for the qualities that they desire in a partner and in their relationships. I am fully aware that any woman I am attracted to or even involved with might, at some point, be attracted to someone else for any number of reasons; perhaps someone taller, or wealthier, or more attractive, or athletic. She might find someone else she has more laughter with or has more in common...there might be a better match out there for her. That doesn't surprise me nor upset me should this be the case. It is not a blow to my self-esteem if my partner decides that I am not a good fit for her. I don't think any less of a woman who is not attracted to me or deciders to break up with me. We mustn't allow our self-esteem to hinge on what anyone else thinks about us.

Consider this for a moment: many beautiful models are turned down for ads or roles consistently because they don't have the "look" that the artist or director has in mind. Is it logical that these models feel any less attractive because they were turned down for that that job? I don't think so. Perhaps the director wanted someone older or younger, or less attractive for the part. It makes no sense to take these rejections as a blow to their self-esteem, but I'll bet many of these models do feel bad when they are rejected, because it's a reflex reaction. Our primitive brain responds to these situations by reflexively sending negative thoughts and emotions that are irrational. Here again, is an opportunity to examine our emotions logically, rationally and ask ourselves, "should I really be feeling this way right now?" or "should I really feel any less about myself?"

We must get in the habit of doing this with our relationships. We have to be aware that, in reality, we should not let ourselves feel down even for a moment when these things happen. They are not a reflection on us, our attractiveness, or our worthiness to experience love. Do not let situations like these make you feel less about yourself. These are the lessons that I have learned that I want to share to help others. I've learned to overcome these feelings by simply thinking rationally.

Chapter 8

Sex

I'll keep this section brief, but I have some advice about how soon a couple should engage in sex. If we are looking for a long-term, serious relationship, we shouldn't rush into having sex. We would be playing with fire if we have strong romantic feelings (fallen in love), but not yet had time to develop the deeper evolved love that we have for friends. We would be wise to wait until we have developed mutual respect and trust in one another before engaging in sex. The time to have sex is when the evolved love has developed, and we can both honestly say to each other "no matter what happens with our romance, I will always care about you as a person…as a friend." Then the sex will be amazing! We will have built an incredible bond, and, because we have waited, the anticipation will have built up to an incredible level. We will have trust in each other, and this helps to free us from fear. From my own experiences, even after the evolved love has developed between partners, I think it's ideal to spend the first night together without having sex. Trust me! Just cuddle, talk, and sleep together. I find that we develop a stronger bond and have a much deeper connection if we refrain from intercourse the first night in bed together. If it feels right, perhaps have sex the next morning…I think couples will have a much better sexual experience having spent the night refraining from sex.

Chapter 9

Consciously Examine Your Emotions

I've talked a little bit about the idea that we must make it a practice to consciously think about the emotional responses that we feel and evaluate whether those impulses are justified and how we should respond to them. In order to do that, I believe we must get into a habit of asking ourselves these questions: *Why am I feeling this way? Is it logical for me to feel this way?* I think you will find as I have, that many of our kneejerk emotional responses in life are totally irrational. Once you determine that the emotion is irrational…it should significantly weaken in power automatically, if not completely fade away. Mastering the ability to consciously examine one's emotions rather than reacting to them impulsively is a huge step toward breaking the shackles that have been enslaving you to your emotions. Emotions happen reflexively, but we have the power to either pay attention to them and act in response to them, or lessen the intensity of those emotions, and even override them with our intellect, if we can convince ourselves intellectually that our emotional response is not justified or irrational. This skill comes easier and more intuitively for some, but I believe we each have it within us to be able to do this on regular basis. It takes practice. But the first step toward mastery is becoming conscious of our ability to do this.

What I have found in my life is that focusing logically and rationally on my emotions is like focusing the rays of the sun on the morning mist. Heartbreak and heartache evaporate if we think logically. That is why I am trying to share my thought process and perspectives…so that I may help others. Let me give you a personal example.

One of the breakups that was the hardest for me to handle was with a woman that I actually knew the least over the few dates that we went on. We spent a couple of weekends together and I came into town to visit her again. We went out to a dance club, and we had a falling out. After that night, she basically decided that she didn't want to see me again. My knee-jerk emotional reaction was extreme disappointment and anger toward her. Looking back, I guess I felt that she owed me an explanation, or owed me a second chance.

But as I thought about it rationally, and was trying to be fair to her, I realized that she didn't owe me anything. She was entitled to end the relationship for any reason. She didn't make any promises to me; we weren't even an exclusive couple yet. I had no justification to be upset with her. It was not her fault that I fell so head-over-heels in love. This was a woman that I was EXTREMELY attracted to. Physically, she was my ideal woman, and I loved her energy and sense of humor. She liked the same music and dance clubs that I did. She dressed sexy and she was a great dancer. I fell in love…hard. That night we broke up I remember thinking to myself that I wouldn't want to look at another woman for weeks, I was so disappointed. The breakup took all my enthusiasm for dating and sex away. I was surprised that I was so affected by the breakup, because I realized I really never got to know her that well. So I pondered why on Earth I was feeling so hurt and disappointed about breaking up with a woman I hardly got a chance to know. I didn't have the concept of 'evolved love' back then, but I still realized that my extreme disappointment over the fact that our relationship didn't last was illogical.

I realized that the mistake I made was weaving a whole fantasy in my head about how we were meant to be together because I was so extremely attracted to her. That fantasy I had created became my *expectation* for how the relationship would go and where it would lead. I had bought into the prevailing idea that "when you meet the *right one*, it's such an overwhelming feeling that *you just know* that this is **the one** *you are meant to be with."* This was how I felt about her. I was head over heels, and I mistakenly believed that we were meant to be together. When she ended it, I was angry and bitter. But deep down I knew it wasn't fair for me to be angry at her. I realized that she didn't do anything wrong. She was well within her right to break up with me for any reason, and moreover, I had no reason to be disappointed. I never got a chance to discover what kind of person she was, and the odds are that she wouldn't have had all the qualities I need anyway, and vice versa. Because of my infatuation and the 'wisdom' that had been handed to me, I had weaved an entire fantasy of how we were meant to be together. This is when I fully realized the power of infatuation and lust, and how easy it is to confuse with love. We need to do a better job of warning children and young adults not to confuse lust with love.

Once I had spent a couple of weeks rationally thinking about all of this, and realizing that my emotions were not justified, and illogical, my heartache went away…pretty much automatically. And to this day I do not look back and think about "what might have been…" I have no scars from the relationship, or any other relationship I've been in. This is my point: **once you convince yourself that your emotions are irrational, you can conquer them.**

All it takes is a solid philosophy and understanding of the biology and chemistry of love. Once you are convinced that it makes no sense for you to feel heartbroken, it becomes very easy, almost automatic, to dispel those negative emotions.

If that sounds to you like I'm coming in with a negative attitude or negative expectation, that is not what I'm doing. I'm approaching the relationship with optimism and curiosity and hoping that those qualities will be there in the relationship. I hope that we're going to be a great match and have a great time together. If those qualities are there, great! I want to be in a relationship for as long as those qualities remain. But if I don't find all those qualities that I need, it's not a surprise. It's not shocking or devastating. I don't even feel disappointed; that would be like looking up at the evening sky and being disappointed that was not pink. It is what it is. We must accept it and move on. It's fine for us to be optimistic, but it's also important to be realistic.

And also, knowing that this relationship is not likely going to last a lifetime, even if I find it has all those qualities for the time being, I don't make the common mistake of <u>investing my ego and self-esteem into making the relationship last a lifetime</u>. I think that's one of the <u>biggest mistakes that people make.</u> Just because the relationship doesn't last does not mean there is something wrong with us, or that anything *went* wrong, or that it should be considered a *failure*. Should the day come when one or more of those necessary qualities is no longer present in the relationship, what are we hanging onto? It's okay to let go. There are so many amazing people on this planet to love and to learn from.

When I was young, before I started dating, I imagined that I would probably end up staying with and marrying the first girl I dated. I thought to myself, "I am a nice, patient, understanding guy with a good heart. Any woman that falls in love with me would certainly always stay." To me, in my youth, that was a romantic notion: to go through life loving only one woman. How naïve I was about myself, and about love!

Had I actually married my first girlfriend, I would never have discovered what other levels of happiness, fun and connection are possible in a relationship. If we are ever going to find a great match, we must test the waters out with different people. Otherwise we'll never know the possibilities, and beyond that, you'll never fully understand *yourself*. You will learn different things about yourself through your relationships with different people. And it's only through experience that we can ever figure out what characteristics we want and need a partner to be truly happy.

I was in college when I started dating my first girlfriend. I was definitely attracted to her, and we had fun together. I remember thinking, "this is the girl I want to marry". My concept of marriage is two people in a constant struggle to compromise and find a peaceful middle ground. I imagine two people resigned to the fact that there many things that each might want to do in life that they are willing to sacrifice for the sake of keeping the marriage together. I think it's an admirable to be able to do that, but that's not the kind of life that I want. If my first girlfriend did not have the wisdom and courage to break up with me, I would have sacrificed much of myself to keep that relationship together.

Back then, I didn't love myself. I needed validation. I needed a girlfriend or wife to feel successful as a man. I think we all feel that as young men, and I am sure it's very similar for women but even more intense because of the messages they get from society. Women feel tremendous pressure to settle down and find a husband and have kids, lest they be judged a failure or looked upon with pity. We need to stop doing that to our young men and women—to each other. As a grown man now who knows himself, who has a healthy self-esteem, I would never dream of making those sacrifices for any relationship. I want to do the things in this life that I want to do.

Another concept from pop culture that I think is worth discussing is the idea of being "in the friend zone." Basically, this is when you are attracted to someone romantically, but they don't have the same attraction to you; they only like you as a friend. Pop culture sends a message that this phenomenon should be seen as an embarrassment, disappointment, or insult. I say it shouldn't be taken as any of those things. Again, we can fall in love and have a sexual attraction to someone that we know nothing about, so why should someone take pride in that? Whereas the love that people have for friends is based on getting to know a person's character and respecting their character, which is actually something to take pride in. You should get more satisfaction from having earned the love of friendship, rather than knowing that someone just finds you physically attractive. We must reverse the thinking on this. I think it's an important point to make, to help us get a better handle on relationships and how they can affect our self-esteem.

Let me give you another example of when you might fall in love with someone that you should not pursue. Earlier I talked about the fact that you may not be compatible or good for each other, but here's another example. Women and men will come into your life that you have a strong attraction to and desires for that are off-limits. As an example, your best friend's boyfriend or girlfriend, or your best friend's spouse, or your brother's or sister's spouse, or your child's teacher. Or, if you're a teacher you might "fall in love" with your student. Just because you fell in love, it does not mean that you're meant to be together forever, or should be together for any period of time!

I also want to point out that being attracted to people who it would be inappropriate to assume a relationship with does not make you a *bad* person. Feeling attraction is automatic, and not something you choose. Don't feel guilty or ashamed for any kind of attraction that you have. Attraction is not the issue; it is the actions you take in response to your attraction that will be the issue.

You're not missing out on your "soul mate" because there is no such thing. Relax. You will fall in love again, hopefully with people who it will be appropriate to pursue. Don't leave your partner or spouse simply because you fell in love with someone new. There are good reasons for leaving your partner (if the relationship is not working/not healthy) but this is not one of them.

Chapter 10

"Successful" Relationships

What are the characteristics of a successful relationship? As I alluded to earlier, I think it's absolutely imperative that every man and woman sit down some time, and think about and list the qualities and characteristics that they need in their relationship with their partner in order to feel happy and fulfilled.

When I say requirements, I truly mean *requirements*. If the relationship is lacking in any of these essential areas, you should move on. I refer to this a deal breaker. Just as I said about abusive relationships, a deal breaker doesn't mean you stop loving and caring about that person; it just means you're not going to be happy together, and you should look for other people that will make you happy. The romantic love will fade away, but you can and should still love each other as friends.

These are the criteria that I need to have to meet my definition of a successful relationship:

-We have fun together.

-We make each other laugh.

-We support each other and help each other overcome our struggles; we cheer each other on with our ambitions.

-We inspire each other to become better people.

-We challenge each other to grow to become better people. In other words, we aren't afraid to call each other on our shortcomings, but we do it in a loving, non-judgmental way.

-We share similar values. For example, I could not date a racist.

-We have common interests, and each of us has some different interests.

-We have interesting conversation.

-We communicate effectively, and have similar levels of intelligence, otherwise the relationship is not going to be fun.

-We have great sex.

-We have similar views on starting a family. Whether we both want to have any kids, and, if so, how many kids do we want to have together?

Something I left off my list, that someone else might understandably require, is "sharing similar religious views." I can understand that some might consider this a crucial factor, but not for me.

Here's an important point I want to stress: it's HARD to find all those qualities in another person. You probably won't agree with my list 100%. I may list criteria that wouldn't be a deal breaker for your relationships, and you may require things that I haven't included in my list. That's to be expected because we are all different, but we should all *make our own list,* and understand that we are probably not going to find all those qualities in the first person we fall in love with. In fact, we might not find *any* of those qualities in the first person we fall in love with. It's probably going to take a while, and we'll have to date lots of people before finding these qualities in one person—so let's get out there and look! Let us appreciate the fun and take joy in the process of meeting and getting to know and love people! By having an idea of the qualities that we need, we can effectively evaluate whether our relationship is meeting those requirements.

Further complicating the picture is the reality that we all change as we go through life. Our interests change. Our values change. Sometimes our religious views change. Sometimes we change our mind about whether we want kids are not. I know I have. So we may find someone that meets all our criteria *for a time*, but at some point… things change. Perhaps we no longer have great conversations together. Perhaps we will find that we don't have as much fun together because our interests have changed. It's ok. It doesn't mean that we should be upset with each other or stop caring about each other. It doesn't mean our time together was wasted or that we loved the *wrong* person. We cannot love the wrong person. Everyone is deserving of our love. By understanding that we all change over time, it shouldn't be shocking or upsetting to one day find that the relationship is no longer working. There is no good guy. No bad guy. No need for blame or bitterness toward each other. The friendship should still remain.

I've hinted at this earlier, but let me say it again: *to be truly alive, one must change; one must grow; one must evolve.* I'm reminded of Bob Dylan's lyric, "he not busy being born, is busy dying." I concur with Bob. What happens if we wake up tomorrow with a burning desire to go on an expedition to Antarctica for two years? Should we *expect* our partner or spouse to come with us on the expedition simply because we are a couple? I think that's unfair. Our partner must be free to make a choice about whether they want to come or not, and do so guilt-free. Furthermore, looking at my own life, anyone who might have married me in my 20s would not recognize the person I am today. Back then I was a devout Catholic, I was much more shy and introverted, I considered myself a conservative Republican, I was much more judgmental of others, I didn't like dance music and couldn't imagine going out to a dance club. Back then, I thought I wanted to get married and have children. So much has changed. I don't think the same; I don't behave the same; I don't see the world the same. I no longer ascribe to any organized religion. I am certain I never want to marry, and that is not going to change. At this point in my life I don't expect I'll ever want children…but I know that can *change*. At this point I can't imagine changing my mind about children, I am open to the idea that I might change my mind someday. The reality is that we constantly change throughout life.

In my 20's, I really didn't *know myself*. I was still conforming to what my parents and peers told me I should be, and how I should think. I was still becoming the person I wanted to be. How could I reasonably expect that anyone who married me in my mid-20s would still want to be with me today? Perhaps she would still want to be with me, but I could not be surprised or upset if those drastic changes meant that we no longer had working, successful marriage. I want to make an important point about this list of essential characteristics is that just because we have all those qualities in our relationship *today*, that does not guarantee that those qualities will all be in place *tomorrow*…because we all change. This is one of the main issues I have with the prevailing concept of marriage. To me, marriage seems like an unspoken promise *not to change too much.*

And, at the point that couples are no longer supportive of each other, or at the point that they no longer have great conversations with one another, or at the point that there is abuse…then it's no longer a successful relationship. And so the length of time that a couple has been together really has no place in the equation of determining whether the relationship is successful or not. If we're not having fun together, supporting each other, and helping each other grow…it's not a successful relationship. To me, the relationship is a sham at that point. If we are faking happiness and satisfaction in our relationships, then we are cheating ourselves and our partner out of finding something better and more satisfying. It's ok to break up if we are not happy. It doesn't mean that we should stop caring about each other.

Chapter 11

<u>Cheating</u>

Let's do another thought experiment. Imagine that medical science could extend human lifespan to 500 years (which is a real possibility in the future)… is it realistic to think that we are going to be happy and satisfied by sharing a bed with one person all that time? Is possible that we might get along so well and be so crazy about our partner (and vice versa) that we would want to remain a couple all that time? Think about that…just one person for all that time… Or, is it more realistic to expect that, at some point, we will want to spend some quality time with someone else? What about if we lived 1,000 years…could we be happy with just one person? There's a song by Three Dog Night that says "one is the loneliest number", but I think <u>two is still a pretty lonely number</u>. I think most of us need multiple people to bond with and care about during our lifetime in order to be truly happy and fulfilled.

The way I see it, at some point two people get to know each other so intimately that there's not much to learn from each other anymore…the relationship is less stimulating; and less fun. The spark is basically gone at that point. That doesn't mean we stop loving and caring about each other, it simply means that it would be more fun and enriching for each of us to spend time with someone else. We have new things to learn from new people. We shouldn't be surprised or saddened by this reality. It's completely logical. If we look back at our lives 10 years ago, and consider the friends that we were spending time with…how many of them are we still spending large amounts of time with? We likely still care deeply for those friends from the past, but at some point it's more fun to spend time with new people and have different experiences and be exposed to different perspectives. That's life. I don't find it sad that we move on to new people in life. Ideally we can still find time to spend with our old friends every so often; they need not pass completely out of our life. But I think it is unrealistic to expect that the sparks of friendship are going to sustain happiness over years and years.

How many times have we heard a story along the lines of: happily married couple; husband finds out his wife has been cheating on him; husband gets a gun and kills the woman he "loved". I imagine lots of guys probably hear the stories like this and think "yeah, I imagine that I might do exactly the same thing in his shoes." There are similar stories about girlfriends or wives who discover their partner cheating and react with acts of extreme violence. I think you see where I'm going with this.

These kinds of reactions are totally incompatible with evolved love. We could never intentionally harm someone we cared deeply about, no matter how much pain they may have caused us, or how wronged we may feel. Some might argue that this reaction is not necessarily incompatible with love because this kind of emotional pain could plausibly lead to a state of temporary insanity, and that these acts are committed almost unconsciously in a state of rage. I won't debate whether it is theoretically possible (even though I don't believe it); it would consume too much time and is unnecessary to the point I'm trying to make. Regardless of whether we can entertain doing something similar because cheating is so devastating and painful, let's at least agree that this is not the best way to react to and deal with a partner who cheats.

I want to lay out a philosophy that should help men and women minimize the pain that we are prone to feel upon discovering our partner or spouse has cheated. Why is cheating is so painful for us? Undoubtedly, much of our pain is born of embarrassment. But let's think about this…is it logical to feel embarrassed over a cheating partner? So many of us have come to believe that if a partner strays it reflects poorly on *us* as a person, or as a lover. We seem to think that <u>if only we were good enough, he/she would not even be *tempted* to stray</u>. In reality, the fact that our partner has strayed says *nothing* about our worth or sex appeal. No matter how great, sexy, or beautiful we may be, our partner <u>will be tempted to stray</u>. We could be People Magazine's "Sexiest Man or Woman Alive" and our partner is *still* going to be extremely attracted to other people! It's perfectly natural to be tempted to stray. As mature adults we should be able to accept this, and not feel any less about ourselves because of it. We need to forgive our partners for being human and having attraction to others. We must also forgive ourselves when we feel a temptation to stray. If we are going to minimize the temptation for partners to actually cheat, then we must learn to remove the feelings of guilt associated with temptation. Feelings of guilt only serve to fuel the temptation.

<u>All of us will be tempted</u>. That doesn't mean that we are weak or bad. In fact, <u>we are not a bad people for any thought or emotion that arises within us</u>. Thoughts and emotions don't hurt anyone! We should never feel guilty for being sexually attracted to <u>anyone</u>. It is our *actions* that we must judge ourselves by.

Let me be clear: **I do not condone cheating**. I value honesty and integrity. If we have made a promise to our partner or spouse, we should honor it. If the day comes that we want to have sex with someone else, then we must be honest and candid with our partner, and let the chips fall where they may. Our partner should have the option to either maintain the relationship with us, or break up. But whatever freedom we have, our partner should also have. The rights and freedoms that couples enjoy in a relationship must be shared 50/50.

In answer to my earlier question: there is no logical reason to feel embarrassed over a cheating partner. <u>The fact that our partner has cheated reflects 100% on our **partner's character**</u>. We shouldn't be asking ourselves "what's wrong with me?" "Why wasn't I enough for him/her?" The reality is that no person who has ever walked the earth is *so* sexy and *so* wonderful that their partner won't be tempted to have sex with someone else Of course they will be tempted, even if only for the sake of being with someone new…even if the new partner is much less attractive. Once again, I must point out: **our brains crave *novelty***. Understanding that a cheating partner doesn't reflect on us should make it much easier for us to handle our emotions after learning of an infidelity. We shouldn't let it rock our world.

I think the flip side of the coin is also true. The fact that our partner *does not cheat*, is not reflection on us either. It doesn't mean that we are such a hot commodity, or that we are so great and sexy that no one would have a reason or temptation to cheat on us. The truth we must accept is: no one will ever be that into us. Just the idea of a new sexual partner will always be alluring. It's a mistake to build our ego on the idea that our partner would never be tempted to cheat. The fact that our partner doesn't cheat reflects 100% on the character of our partner; not on our desirability as a mate.

I have a theory as to why some men and women cheat leading up to their wedding, sometimes even the night before. I'm not saying this a common, but it happens. I think can be explained by two factors. First is the realization that "this could be the last time I get a chance to be with someone else. I'd better take advantage of the opportunity." But I think there's a second factor that most have not considered that is an even more likely culprit: Fear. Men and women often cheat as a way to protect their heart (sorry, there's that false paradigm again). We can be so overtaken by the power of being in love (primitive love), that we can have an unconscious fear of giving our heart 100% to our spouse for fear of vulnerability and heartbreak. If we can cheat on our wedding night, then we have put up a wall of protection. Again, I stress the point that fear and love do not mix. There is an inverse relationship between the two. We must master our fear if we are to love and live fully.

I can tell you from personal experience, I've felt this same temptation creeping up from my subconscious when I was falling madly in love. I was confused by the realization that some part of me might want to cheat on someone that I was crazy about and truly loved. So I did some self-reflection, and realized that it was my unconscious trying to protect me. If I had sex with another woman it would protect me from falling too "head over heels" for one woman. I recognized it for what it was, and decided I didn't want to do *anything* to dampen the intensity of my attraction to my partner; but it dawned on me that this same phenomenon probably explains a lot of the stories I've heard (sometimes celebrity stories) of a bride or groom cheating right before their wedding. I don't think it's done out of disrespect, or out of cruelty, but rather as a protective move motivated by an unconscious fear. The lesson again: we must conquer our fears if we are to give love in a healthy, authentic way.

Chapter 12

Breaking Up

I didn't realize it at the time, but one of the greatest days of my life was the day that my first girlfriend broke up with me, because it opened the door for me to date a lot of women and figure out who I am and what I want in life. At that time in my life I lacked confidence in myself. I doubted that I could be successful attracting and dating women, and regretfully thought that I might have to settle and marry a woman that I was not crazy about. Let me say this loud and clear: <u>none of us should have to settle for relationships that do not make us extremely happy and satisfied</u>.

When my first girlfriend broke up with me, I found myself asking questions like "what's wrong with me?" "Why am I so unlovable?" "What should I change about myself so that I can be loved?" I suppose these are typical questions when we are young and going through our first experiences and breaking up. It's always good to ask some questions after a breakup and think about what we might do differently in our future relationships. However, as I have gotten older and wiser I realize there are better questions I could've been asking myself. For example, just because one person decided to break up with me, did that mean there was something wrong with me? When we are young and immature I think we are quick to make this assumption. With maturity, hopefully, we come to understand that partners will have lots of valid reasons for breaking up with us that are not character faults or personality issues.

In the case of my first girlfriend, she told me one of the reasons that she broke up is because I wasn't in a *serious* mood often enough.

It bothered her that I was always happy and in a jovial. She wanted to see me be serious more often. At that young age, I took that to heart. I actually started to question myself, "maybe I need to be more serious!" "Why am I such a goofball?! "I need to work on being more serious all the time!"

After years of thinking this way, I finally realized: I don't want to change anything about who I am just for the sake of making a relationship last longer. To me, that is the ultimate fail. I want to approach life and relationships in my own way; to be myself, and enjoy the relationship for as long as it lasts.

Let me make this clear: there was nothing wrong with her wanting to be with someone who is was more serious. She's entitled to look for that, and I can't judge her for it, or be mad at her for wanting someone like that, or for breaking with me over it. The bottom line was that <u>we just weren't a good match</u>. Most of the people we get involved with are not going to be a good match. If I am not a good match for anyone, it's not upsetting to me. I can handle it. I want to know that anyone that I get romantically involved with has the same self-esteem and maturity.

I want to know that I have the freedom to leave for any reason that I see fit, and she is still going to be fine. Moreover, that she loves me enough to let me do that. Yes, we might miss each other. Of course. However, we're not going to make the mistake of thinking that this relationship "defines us", "makes us complete," is going to give us "heaven," or that the other person "is the one that we were meant for/is our soul mate." We are not going to think that we found "that one special love that's magic and last forever." It's precisely this kind of thinking that gets us into trouble. The evidence that love does not work this way is all around us.

Also, I have to talk about those songs and movies that paint a romantic picture of a man or woman pining away for the "love of a life" who can't be here because of circumstances beyond their control. And so they pine away alone, and spend their days in misery and longing, rather than getting out and sharing love with someone else. It's fine to be sexually faithful, but what's the point of staying home alone and being sad? There's someone else out there who needs love too. Love is not a precious commodity. It is abundant and meant to be shared. If the "love of your life" makes it back some day, you will find that love will still be there. There's no need to waste our days in misery and solitude.

"How will I know if it's love? I can't tell you, but it lasts forever"

—**"When it's Love", Van Halen**

I think this line by Van Halen basically encapsulates the wisdom we keep passing down and repeating even with all the evidence to the contrary. We really do a disservice to everyone to repeat the same wisdom, because it creates a false expectation, disillusionment and confusion when it inevitably fades out. And now, rather than appreciating the time that you had, you look at that time spent together as a waste, or that it wasn't real, they were just using you are playing you. "He/she was must have been lying to me!"

Once we start drawing conclusions like this it becomes mental and emotional baggage, and puts up obstacles to entering a new healthy relationship in the future. Those that think this way become jaded and put up barriers to love, if they are even open to trying again. Some people just give up. We've got to do better. Start to accept and understand that love can be real and beautiful and rewarding but it doesn't necessarily mean the relationship is guaranteed to work forever. Maybe it will work forever. I'm just saying it's not necessarily guaranteed, nor is it a waste of time. So go in fearlessly. There's nothing to fear but fear itself, as Franklin D. Roosevelt said. Fear becomes the blockade to love.

I think a lot of men and women, and certainly younger people, really are unsure whether or not they actually do love their partner. How can we know if it's love?...

The Love Test: A Thought Experiment

It is fairly easy to recognize when we have fallen in love with someone. It's instinctual, reflexive, usually automatic, and there are some clear signs to look for as I've covered earlier. But it's important that we also have a way to know whether we also love our partner in the evolved/divine sense/unconditional sense, and we want to have a way to make sure our partner loves us the same way. I have created a simple thought experiment so that we can get some insight into the nature of our feelings:

Let us imagine that our partner meets someone tomorrow that they have more chemistry and fun with. What if our partner is happier being with someone else?...

If we don't love our partner enough to let them go—if we can't still care deeply and love them as a friend even after they have left us for someone new…then we do not love our partner in the healthy, evolved sense; it is our primitive/selfish love that we are

<u>allowing to rule our mind</u>. Also, if we can't let our partner go then we do not love ourselves! When we truly love ourselves, we only want to be in a relationship with someone who wants to be with *us!* Loving ourselves means that we would never ask someone to be with us out of pity, or out of a sense of *obligation.*

If we can't allow our partner that kind of freedom, then we have mistakenly bought into the idea that our partner somehow validates us as men and women. We have mistakenly come to think that our partner makes us complete. If we cannot let our partner go and love them all the same then our relationship is not based on friendship, respect, how much we *care* about our partner and *their happiness,* but instead based on how our partner *makes us feel*…we are letting the selfish/primitive parts of our brain rule our minds. It's not healthy. Primitive love can be thought of loving with a <u>closed fist</u>, in attempt to possess; evolved love can be thought of loving with an open hand. The presence of evolved love does *not* erase the presence of primitive love, it simply *overrides* it. It is a conscious choice we have the power to make. We may still have desire to be with our partner, but more importantly, we want them to be happy and free.

I really think we'd all be much better off if we recognize that we cannot be angry at someone else for breaking up with us, as long as they are being honest. As free and independent persons we all have the right to pursue happiness in this life. We all ought to be allowed to break up for any reason we deem important. I can understand some might be angry if they suspect their partner only got involved for sex or for money, but in that case we shouldn't be upset over the *break up;* we should be upset over the nature of the relationship. The break up in this case would *be good* news. When we break off a romantic relationship it doesn't necessarily mean we care any less for the other person, it simply means the relationship wasn't working. Consider this: we care deeply for our closest friends, correct? We love them as friends. Does it mean that our friends would make great romantic partners for us? Does it mean that we want to see them every day? ...for months and years on end? I know that lots of people are averse to dating their friends, for fear that, if the romance doesn't work out, the friendship would be lost as well. It doesn't have to be this way. With the right frame of mind, the friendship should still remain, even after a romantic split. It can be done. The reality is that it's extremely difficult to find long-term compatibility with anyone. And so we should not be shocked to one day realize the relationship is no longer working; it is no longer satisfying. It doesn't mean there is anything wrong with either of us.

Moreover, realize that just because it didn't last doesn't mean the love wasn't *real*, or that the time together was somehow wasted. Armed with a better understanding of the nature of romantic/primitive love, we can now enjoy it fearlessly. We can appreciate it, and soak it up while it's in our life. And when it's gone, we will have the satisfaction that we fully savored and experienced it. We will have enjoyed the roller coaster ride together, and treasure the memories of it.

Chapter 13

Divorce

In any relationship, should either partner decide that the relationship is no longer working for them, they should be free to go. We cannot fault them. We cannot blame them for wanting to be happy. We each have our own lives to live. Life is short; we should be free to pursue happiness while we are here. Again, just because the romantic relationship didn't work out, it doesn't mean that we must stop caring about each other. If couples grew to care deeply about each other, then friendship and mutual caring should still be intact after a romantic split.

One of the challenges that we have in shifting our views on marriage and divorce is that no one wants to let their marriage problems show, except with our closest friends. Many dread the social stigma of divorce, or don't like the idea of divorce because of their religious views. I think it is extremely important that we collectively make an effort to remove the social stigma still often associate with divorce. Why should there be any stigma? We know that marriages don't always work out no matter how hard couples try. People change. I am extremely conscious of what I say when I find out that a friend is going through a divorce. I don't even express pity; I express a sincere congratulation, and I explain why. I think it's safe to say that couples do not get divorced unless they are extremely unhappy…and we all deserve to be happy. I think it takes more courage and honesty to get divorced than to get married.

As a young boy I would imagine what my life would be like as an adult. I would try imagine what it is like to be married. It occurred to me how awful it would be to find myself in a loveless marriage, just going through the motions. Because of my religious upbringing, I knew I would never choose to get divorced, so I imagined finding myself stuck; an actor playing the part of a happy husband.

I've tried to get an accurate statistic of the divorce rate in the United States, but I found a lot of disparity in the figures I found. Most people seem to accept that about half of all marriages end in divorce, but whether it is 30% or 60%, the point is, we all know plenty of people that have been divorced. More than that, we all know plenty of people who are miserable in their current marriage and yet stick it out. We also know plenty of people who may not be *miserable*, but they are not *deeply satisfied* with their marriage. I think we all deserve to be deeply happy. I imagine many, many men and women are reluctant to speak candidly to their spouse and honestly express their dissatisfaction in the marriage, because they don't want to hurt them. On top of that, I'm sure there are many, many men and women who aren't understand why they are feeling dissatisfied, and would therefore have difficulty communicating about it. To me, it's clear we have an issue to address.

Something I've come to realize over the course of my life is that the vast majority of us would sooner believe that there is something wrong with *us*, than to question the validity of our existing paradigms. The paradigm that has been handed down is that one day we will meet The One we are meant to be with, we'll be blown away with an intense experience of falling in love, get married and then live happily ever after. But the evidence is everywhere that this is a bogus paradigm, and it leads to confusion, heartache, and fear. Why do couples choose to get divorced? These are people who were so sure of their love for each other that they got up in front of friends, family, and God…and promised to stay together; to honor and cherish each other, and forsake all others…for the rest of their lives. Yet so many are divorced within a few years—sometimes within a few weeks. They're so unhappy and unfulfilled they will bear the cost and "shame" of getting a divorce.

As a society, we have tried our utmost to ensure that couples enter marriage with the deepest respect and commitment, and that these couple is intent on making it work come hell or high water. It's not working. There's something fundamentally wrong here. We may be completely in love and convinced our love will burn forever; but we *can never truly know how you will feel tomorrow*. It is **the promise/the commitment itself that is the issue**. I don't want to hear my partner say, "I will love you forever". I prefer to hear "I love you right now". That is enough, and it means so much more to me than the promise of forever because it's more honest. We don't know how long love lasts. Recognizing this, we can now fully experience and appreciate Right Now.

I have laid a lot of the blame for our collective misconceptions about love on the popular music, but I want to cite a pop song from the 1980s that really nailed the crux of the problem. That song is "Enjoy the Silence" by Depeche Mode. "… *vows are spoken to be broken. Feelings are intense; words are trivial….words are very unnecessary; they can only do harm.*" It's the spoken promise that can never honestly be made: to stay together. It is the broken promise that gets people so upset and hurt. How many songs have you heard about the idea of "broken promises"? But if we stop to think about it…**what are we committing to? Are we are committing to stay together even when we are not happy**? If that is the commitment, let's be clear about it at the outset. But my question is, "why would we make that commitment?"

When a relationship is working and couples are happy together, **there is no need for commitment**. If we're not happy, why would we stay together? I can think of one answer. We might reasonable commit to stay together, even if we aren't happy together, for the sake of raising a family. I can understand that, but let's be honest about this from the get-go. For a couple that doesn't want to start a family together, what's the point of getting married? Tax benefits? Insurance benefits? Ok, but at the point that we're not happy together, there should be no hesitation about separating. We deserve to be happy; and if one of us is not happy, the other cannot be happy if we care about each other. The obvious truth that I feel compelled to point out is that we can care deeply about our partner (and vice versa) and simply not be a good fit for each other. It's common. There's nothing to be upset about.

Chapter 14

Marriage

"If I were painting a picture of the primal couple (Adam and Eve), I would not put wedding clothes on them. As a matter of fact, the original artist put no clothes on them. The point of the story was not to get them married, but to get them going on their adventure. No wedding gowns, no tuxedos. No vows, no certificates. Just two naked people, leaning on each other, trying to make sense of their surroundings and the meaning of their lives. Two people, trying to understand their relationship to God while also trying to figure out how to be companions to each other."

First Comes Love? The Ever-Changing Face of Marriage, John C. Morris

I've already laid out some of my issues with marriage, but a topic of this magnitude deserves its own chapter.

I remember years ago talking with a coworker about the idea of marriage. At that time of my life I was starting to conclude that marriage probably wasn't something I would be interested in trying. When he found out I wasn't keen to the idea of marriage he asked, "Doug, don't you want someone to clean the house and cook for you while you are at work all day?" I thought about it for a second and replied, "No. I don't care about that at all. I want someone that I can have fun with!" He was taken aback, as if that thought never occurred to him before. People think about relationship differently…

Let me say this: as long as two people are honest about their intentions, their desires, and expectations, and want to get married, of course I wish them well and hope they have lasting happiness together. But I think it's imperative that any couple, married or not, recognize: **this relationship *may not* work out for the long term.** Each give it your best shot, and try to make it work, but *if it doesn't* work out—if we're not *truly* happy and satisfied—there shouldn't be shock, horror, or shame; no vilifying of either party—and try to keep the friendship intact. Friendship /evolved love is the more beautiful version of love because it comes without strings, and it doesn't degrade into bitterness and hatred.

I think we need to flip the entire paradigm of Love on its head. The existing paradigm of love is based on the selfish impulses and desires of our primitive/reptilian brains, but we aren't reptiles any longer. Our species has evolved, and all of the noblest ideals that we celebrate as a species: equality, fairness, justice, living in peace and harmony, and divine/unconditional love originate in our cerebral cortex. The existing paradigm of commitment, possession and marriage satisfies our selfish reptilian brain; it is the ultimate expression of primitive love...but it *does not satisfy* our evolved brain; our evolved nature. I realize this is a shocking and controversial conclusion, and I don't expect everyone to agree, but I think that my views will make sense to a lot of people. Even for those who disagree with my conclusions, I sincerely hope that my perspectives and scientific insights will help you improve the quality of your relationships.

Some will accuse me of going against thousands of years or tradition, but actually, I am not. The concept of marriage has constantly evolved over the centuries. It wasn't until the last 200 years or so that men and women started thinking of marriage in terms of equality and love. Up until then marriage was typically used as a means to transfer property, build alliances, and gain power.

Again, my definition of evolved love is: **the deepest level of caring about another person. When we care so much that person that they feel like they are a part of us. When we have this level of caring, no matter how much we want to be with them, ultimately we want them to be happy...even if they are happier with someone else.** The concept of marriage is completely incompatible with my definition of love. This is why I will never get married. I would never attempt to put *shackles* on anyone, let alone someone that I cared about. I would never ask someone to stay with me who wasn't happy being with me, because I want them to be happy! I want everyone to by happy, especially those that I love. I think it's also worth pointing out that I don't want a relationship of mediocrity. I want a **fantastic** relationship with someone who is crazy about me, and **actually <u>wants</u> to be with me**! I have one life to live, and I want to enjoy it. Don't we all?

"If you love somebody; if you love someone...set them free" -**Sting**

Back in Chapter 11 I pointed out that we all change over time in multiple ways, and we need to be free to change if we are going to live full and satisfying lives. This is one of the reasons I don't think the prevailing concept of marriage works. In my eyes, marriage implies a promise <u>not to **change** too much</u>.

It's a sad thought for me to imagine having gone through life loving only one woman. The truth is, I loved every woman I've ever been involved with. I fell in love, and I cared deeply. In each case, the time simply came when one or the other realized that we just weren't a good match as a romantic couple. To this day I love them still; I still care deeply about all of them----I still love them as friends. I wish them all the best things in life. But loving them as friends doesn't mean that we're going to be happy together as a couple. In the same way, I care deeply for the female friends that I've made in my life----I think they are great, but we wouldn't make a good romantic couple. Here is how it works: we can experience profound primitive/romantic love for someone we hardly know, but without developing evolved love, our relationship is on truly shaky ground. Conversely, we can develop profound evolved love for someone without having the primitive/romantic love, in which case we have friendship. The key to wonderful romantic relationship is to have **both the *emotion* of primitive and the *thought* of evolved love present**, and each partner **recognize that the evolved love is more important, more selfless**. Should the romance fade, evolved love should still bond couples as friends.

I hope that people will read this book and be motivated to sit down and talk with their partner, and be **candid** with one another. I hope they ask each other if they are *truly* happy in the relationship, and ask if there areas of the relationship that can be improved? Or, are there issues in the relationship that either feels are deal-breakers? We all deserve to be happy. Life is short. If couples find that they are really not happy together, they should consider splitting up---- without guilt or hard feelings. If your significant other finds aspects of the relationship that prevent them from being happy that doesn't mean there is anything wrong with you, nor wrong with them for feeling that way. If it's fixable, fix it. If not, accept that it is what it is. We're not going to be everyone's cup of tea. As mature adults, we must know that, and be ok with it. We must love ourselves, and know that we deserve to be in amazing relationships with partners who truly appreciate our qualities and truly enjoy spending time with us.

I conclude that romantic love, being "in love," can never be promised to anyone into the future. If two people get married believing that they are going to stay *in love* for the rest of their lives; that they are never going to fall in love with anyone else or have desire to be with anyone else…they are mistaken. That's not how it works. The chemical reactions of falling/being in love, and all the related physiological and psychological manifestations that we experience last no more than 18-30 months. Know that. I think it's fair to say that most men and women have been conditioned to believe that romantic love lasts forever, and because of this misconception they agree to get married and are ultimately disappointed when the romance is gone. I think this is why you see the high rate of divorce, cheating, disillusionment, and dissatisfaction in marriages…and men and women second-guessing whether or not they picked the right spouse when the passion is gone.

The biggest reason so many men and women enter their marriage confidently committing for a lifetime is because they bought into this pervasive fairytale notion, that when you meet "the one," your "soul mate," the one you are "meant to be with," you will have a feeling so strong that *you just know* that this is the one that you will love for the rest of your life, the person that you cannot be without. If we believe that romance lasts forever, then it's natural to conclude that marriages that ended in divorce, infidelity, or simply stay together unhappily were a "mistake" from the outset. They either married the wrong person, or someone did something wrong that killed the love; as I discussed in detail in my chapter about the clichés of love. The result is that we have couples looking to blame each other, often times lashing out at each other about how each contributed to the "failed marriage." Or (equally as regrettable) blame themselves when a relationship runs its course, and carry the burden of guilt for the failure. Thus couples spend countless hours in fruitless, masochistic exercises of reliving all the things that they might have done to destroy the marriage, and destroy the love. There is no need for this.

I am sure that the vast majority of partners enter into marriage with the best of intentions: to love each other, support each other, and be happy. People do the best they can to make the marriage work and still be true to themselves, and strive for the things that they want out of life. However, we've created an *expectation that reality could never live up to*. It was simply a lack of understanding about biology, psychology (our complex nature), and love itself…this has lead to our confusion and suffering. We need to fix this.

Can we still defend the institution of marriage? Possibly, but I think we have to rethink marriage a little bit, and adjust our expectations in marriage. For those who decide that they would still like to give marriage a try, I think a different mindset is called for. We need to be realistic. We need to understand that the "in love" part of the relationship, the romance, will fade over time. We must also understand there will be other people that come into their lives that we will be attracted to; perhaps even fall in love with. We must accept that, and make the decision before getting married that we are willing to forgo pursuing those other love interests for the sake of having a partner though life. The foundation of the relationship is not the romance/primitive love, but rather the evolved/unconditional love of friends. The agreement should be that "we're going to support and take care of each other as friends, even if/when the romance has faded". That is a reasonable expectation, and I can understand how two people could still agree to marriage under these circumstances.

But notice, if it's essentially the love of friends that remains after the romance fades, then we should allow each other the same kind of freedom that we allow our other friends. We don't get jealous when our friends want to be alone or spend time with other people. We don't expect our friends to cherish our company at all times. We love our friends but most of us also need some time apart, lest we get bored, or worse, get on each other's nerves.

It's important that if we choose to marry, we be as honest as possible, and set realistic expectations as possible. Making a marriage work is difficult! We must clearly define for ourselves, and be clear with one another about what our definition of a 'working' marriage entails. If couples cannot define it, and explain to one another…it's guaranteed that the marriage won't 'work'. Take the time to discuss it at the outset. Realize that there will be days that the last person on earth we want to see is the one we wake up next to. Expect that these days will come, but be optimistic that these rough patches are temporary, and in those times let us reflect on the thoughts and feelings of respect and caring that we have for your partner—that we are willing to deal with those inevitable moments for the sake of having a partner in life.

We must also anticipate and prepare for those times that we will be sexually tempted to stray. Let us make the conscious decision before getting married that that sexual desire for a new partner will not override or trump the more precious, stronger bond of love that we have for our spouse. Let us make the sober commitment to ourselves that we are willing to deal with feelings of frustration or regret over a lost opportunity that result from resisting the urge to get involved with other sexual partners. Let's face reality: the urge to have sex can be extremely powerful and difficult to resist. I made the point earlier, but it's worth repeating: if the urge to mate wasn't so powerful, <u>none</u> of us would be here today. Even if we are able to resist the urge, we must realize that there will be part of our brain that is kicking us for passing up the chance to satisfy that urge.

If we choose to marry, knowing what we know about the nature of love/romance, then we need to update the concept of marriage with a more thorough understanding of what we are getting into, what to expect, and how we will act. With a deeper understanding of love, we can now get more realistic about our expectations from relationships and marriage.

I call my definition of love, "the new love paradigm", but I say "new" love with a sense of irony; it's not really a new idea. In truth, my paradigm is modeled on the most religious and spiritual teachers have espoused over the centuries. I'm not a religious person, but I love the central message of Jesus, for instance. He was a great example of a human being. He was a man who taught that we should love everyone and forgive everyone, and not judge others. That is exactly how I feel. Can you imagine that Jesus would have a special love for one woman that was more powerful and deeper than his love for humanity? Is that idea compatible with who he was said to be? I don't think that it's compatible. I can't imagine that he would have a deeper love for one woman or person that was deeper than his love for the world. Isn't the ideal, then, to have that care, compassion and love for everyone?

Again, my definition of divine love/evolved love: the deepest level of caring about someone else; when you care so much about that person that you feel that they are part of you. When they are happy, you share and sense that happiness within you. And when they are sad, you are sad; you share and sense a feeling of sadness too. It's the way that a parent naturally loves their child, because they instinctively recognize, understand, and feel that their child is a *part* of them. When you love someone this way ultimately you want two things: you want them to be happy, and you want them to be free to do what they want to do in this life.

"When you care so much about someone that they *feel like they are part of you*"... **love doesn't get any deeper than this**. Love only goes *so* deep. I love my family this way, and I love my closest friends this way. I can't love a partner any deeper than I could love my friends or family. It is only a different *flavor* of love we have for our partner, because there is sexual chemistry. Primitive love adds an extra dimension, but it's not a deeper or stronger love than that of our friends and family. Some might want to argue this point with me, but if someone asked you, "who do you love *more*: your spouse or your parents? ...your spouse or your children?...your lover or your best friend?" Could you make a choice? ...Love only goes so deep.

Using the example of a parent's love for their child, let us consider those cases of parents who at one time viewed homosexuals as bad, evil people, either because of religious teaching or because of society's bias against people who are different. They condemned anyone who was gay and wouldn't have anything to do with them...until they realized that their own child was gay----and it forced them to reevaluate their feelings about gay people. Sadly, not all parents are able to see the light, and they still condemn gay people at the expense of the relationship they have with their child. But most parents have a change of heart when they realize their own child is gay. It is the *perfect love* that a parent has for their child that makes them realize their condemnation of gay people is incompatible with love. Loving their child means they want their child to be **happy and free**. Loving another person means them to have the freedom to love and be with the person they want to be with…to be happy. Organized religions often stress the importance of loving people, but simultaneously try to tell people how they should think and what they should do. That is **not love.** I will not equivocate: **loving another person mandates that we allow them freedom to think, do, and speak as they wish, and love who they wish (as long as they aren't hurting anyone else; it is between consenting adults.)** When I told my mother that I left the Catholic faith, one the points that I made to her is that: "I love people. I want them to be happy and free. I can't love people *and* love the church at the same time".

The ultimate expression of evolved love is *letting go*. Primitive love can be thought of as a clenched fist; "evolved love" can be thought of as an open hand. We must distinguish between these two concepts of love, recognize them and their differences, and put these two concepts of love in the proper perspective. Once we do, everything changes.

This is what I have realized, and it has freed me from the fear of heartbreak. I have no fear when I am falling in love; I experience only excitement and gratitude for every moment of it. I want the whole world to experience love this way. Love is not something to withhold and is not something to fear. You cannot love the "wrong" person. Everyone is worthy, and deserving of love.

Evolved love is the recognition of our connection to someone else. We are all connected, though we often don't seem to recognize it. We don't often think about or sense this truth. However, one of the greatest minds in the history explained it beautifully:

> "A human being is a part of the whole, called by us
> "universe", a part limited in time and space. He experiences
> himself, his thoughts and feeling as something separated
> from the rest, a kind of optical delusion of his consciousness.
> This delusion is a kind of prison for us, restricting us to our
> personal desires and to affection for a few persons nearest to
> us. Our task must be to free ourselves from this prison by
> widening our circle of compassion to embrace all living
> creatures and the whole of nature in its beauty."   ----
> Albert Einstein

The truth is, we've all evolved from a common ancestor; all human beings, and all living creatures. We are all family. It just seems to be much easier to recognize this truth when we get to know someone personally. Whether we sense it or not, we must consciously accept this truth, constantly reflect on it, and live accordingly…we must treat each other accordingly. This divine/evolved love is what we should strive for and celebrate in our culture. **This is the strongest bond that two people can share.** When we share each other's successes and failures, and sense each other's joys and pains as you do your own. When you feel this way about someone, would you try to *shackle* them to you? Would you attempt to *possess* them? Would a loving parent selfishly insist that their child never leave the home and live their own life? If you love someone like that, would you insist that they not go out and have a good time with her friends because you have to stay late at the office? I don't think those behaviors are compatible with this evolved love. When you love someone like this, as much as you *want* to spend time with them, **what matters more... is** *their happiness.*

One of the points I made at the start of this book, is that we all have different desires in life. We have different perspectives and different ideas. Even if you don't agree with my conclusions about marriage and commitment, I hope that my perspective will help you shape your own concepts about what it means to love, and what you hope to get out of your relationships. One of the essential questions you need to ask yourself is whether or not you are going to be satisfied, fulfilled, and happy being in a committed relationship when the romance is gone. Imagine that you have an excellent partner that you respect, and love as you love your own family. Imagine that your relationship ticks all the boxes of criteria you're looking for in a relationship…but you've spent so much time together, and you know each other's minds so well. You know each other inside out, and the romance has faded. Now imagine you meet someone new that you fall in love with. Are you willing to forgo pursuing that new relationship for the sake of maintaining the current relationship?

What about the couples that stay happily married their whole life? How is it that some couples stay happily married for so long? To answer these questions, let us consider the answer such couples give when asked what the secret to their successful marriage is. The answer I've always heard is some variation of "I married my best *friend.*" The word "friend" is the key, and it validates everything that I've said about the finite power and lifespan of *romance,* contrasted to the strength and durability of *friendship.* Romance, being in love/primitive love does not last forever. It is the love of friends and family, the evolved version of love that not only is less selfish, but also is not limited in time. It is this kind of love that we must strive for and celebrate as individuals and as a species. Two people can stay happily married, perhaps, but it must be based on friendship, and respect, caring, and they have to be ok with the fact that romance fades. This is not the kind of love that happens at first sight; it must be develop over time, and can only truly be felt and expressed when you know someone intimately---when you know their character, and their values. You have to understand them intimately, and know and respect their heart (even I can't escape using this cliché!).

The Deceivers

I want to point out another important benefit to be gained by putting romantic love in the proper perspective. The reality is that there is, and always has always been a small percentage of the human population that will lie and manipulates to gain power, wealth, and status. These people can be very charming (at first), and adept at tricking others into falling in love with them. They know all the right words to say, but *they lack true empathy* for others. They don't comprehend what it means to love in the evolved sense that I am describing, and they never will. They don't believe in equality. They are arrogant, and they tend to use people. I don't judge people like this because I understand their brains do not function in a normal way. These people do not have a 'conscience' in the normal sense. They are almost exclusively driven by the selfish impulses of the reptilian brain. Only a very small minority of people suffer from this condition, but there are still many of them out there, and you will run into these from time to time. Oprah Winfrey produced a television series called "Who the F*** Did I Marry?" that shows example after example of men and women that have been duped, fallen in love, and ripped off by very charming frauds. These examples just give one more argument as to why you cannot assume that the person you have fallen in love with is going to be a good fit for you, or that you have found your soul mate. Instead, you may have fallen in love with a psychopath. I strongly encourage you to research the condition and the tell-tale signs of psychopathy. I have known several in my lifetime, including a close friend who I care deeply for. There are several terms that basically describe the same thing: psychopath/sociopath/narcissist. These people are not 'monsters'; they are human beings. I have deep empathy for them. Psychopathy is real, and it's actually rather easy to recognize once we understand the traits and behaviors. I have seen estimates range between 1-4% of the population that have this type of brain. Through the use of PET scans and fMRI scans we can see the psychopaths do not have typical brain activity in the prefrontal cortex, which means they do not have a "conscience" in the way that most of us do. They do not have the same inner struggle that most of us face between our selfish, primitive brain and our evolved, altruistic brain. They are excellent liars because they don't experience feelings of guilt. They can easily beat any lie detector machine. Psychopaths often lie pathologically. I'm convinced that much of human history can be explained by understanding the role that psychopaths have played in humanity's story. Psychopaths are motivated largely by greed; greed for money and greed for power. Think of the phrase "unconscionable greed"…again, psychopaths have no conscience. We can't judge them for their greed, any more that we can judge someone for their height. Their greed often churns the wheels of industry, so psychopaths have a role to play in society. We must re-humanize them and learn not to judge of fear them. Psychopaths tend to view life as a competition rather than a collaborative effort. "He who dies with the most toys, wins" is often how a psychopath thinks. They are much more likely to be politicians and CEOs than serial killers. Politicians who will say anything to get into office…explained by psychopathy. Humanity really needs to stop electing these people to office. We should not allow this minority to sour our faith in human goodness, but would be wise not to deny their existence. Be wary of anyone who insists that you trust them before they have earned it. If you are involved with someone like this, and they are making you miserable, do not hope that they will change. They won't change. Wish them well with their life and get away.

Chapter 15

The Winning Formula

If primitive love and evolve love are both wonderful and yet so different, how can we reconcile the two and find real happiness? Simple. We must unite them. In the same way that our reptilian brain and cerebral cortex find harmony, we must find harmony and balance with the two concepts of love. In essence, we must reconcile the *emotion* of love (primitive love) with the *thought* of love (evolved love). This is where we find the magic: love without strings or fear. Evolved love is essentially the same love that you have for friends and family, but if we are going to love someone else in a healthy and fearless way, we must also have this kind of love for our partner, underlying and superseding the primitive, possessive, romantic love. Without the romantic feelings of being "in love", what we have is just friendship. When we have primitive/romantic love without also having the evolved love, it's unhealthy, selfish, scary, out of control, and will undoubtedly turn to bitterness, jealousy, and disappointment when the romance fades.

When we blend the primitive love with the evolved love, and recognize the supremacy of evolved love... this is the winning formula for a great relationship. We must learn to recognize when our feelings equate primitive love. Again, the symptoms of primitive love, "falling in love," are feelings of excitement, a quickened heartbeat, constantly thinking about the other person, the butterflies in your stomach, and the fireworks...wanting to possess someone because of the way they make you feel...all things that are wonderful and make you feel alive. But we must be cognizant that just because that person that sets off those automatic reactions they may not be a good match for us, and we cannot have evolved love for someone until we get to know them, and respect them…until we *care* so much for them that they feel like a part of us. **Beyond our selfish desire to be with them (no matter how strong), you must love them enough to let them go should they choose.**

I have criticized the fairy tale concept of "happily ever after" but there is one fairy tale that actually shows an excellent example of evolved/unconditional love----"Beauty and the Beast." At what point in the story did the Beast demonstrate that he loved Belle—that he *truly* cared about her? It was the point when he released her from his castle so she could be with her father. As much as he wanted Belle to stay (and needed her to break the spell that kept him in his monstrous form), he chose to give her freedom. **He loved her enough to <u>let her go</u>**. And naturally, she came back to him. By freeing her, he proved to Belle that he loved her…he put her happiness above his selfish desires to be with her. In return, he received confirmation of *her love for him*, because she did return. There was no need for either of them to doubt that their love for each other was pure and selfless. Regardless of how much he wanted her to stay, his ultimate desire was to see her be happy and free…and he was rewarded. This is the beauty of the new love paradigm.

If two people want to get married, I wish them all the happiness in the world. But in my opinion, the concept of marriage is entirely incompatible with evolved love; even if it's with the adjusted expectations that the friendship is going to be the thing that sustains the marriage. I think an open door to leave is a requirement to keep the relationship healthy and fun. This is why I will never get married, but it is also one of the reasons I have no fear of pursuing love, falling in love, expressing love, and no fear of heartbreak. I'm not opposed to the idea that I might find someone that I could be happy with for the rest of my life, but I still wouldn't want to make a commitment to stay together. The commitment automatically kills much of the magic of a relationship. If you want to take the fun out of an activity, make it an *obligation*. A relationship is only a living, breathing thing when there is no commitment or expectation of staying together for any amount of time.

"It's only in uncertainty that we're naked and alive"

—Peter Gabriel, *That Voice Again*

The best, healthiest kind of love that I have experienced is loving someone enough to be able to look them in the eye and say fearlessly "I am in love with you, but more importantly *I love you*; I care deeply for you. I think you are awesome and I am honored to be your friend! I am crazy about you, and love being with you…but, as much as I want to be with you, what's more important to me is that **I want you to be happy**…even if that means you are happier with someone else." If we can honestly express that sentiment to someone we love *and not ask for anything in return*…that is evolved love. My love for someone else is not dependent on how they feel about me. This is the kind of love we should strive for and celebrate.

When we are in a relationship that has all the factors that we are looking for, there is no need for a commitment…that's the person we want to be with. Perhaps counter-intuitively, the fact that both partners are free to go and still be loved, supported, and cared for propels couples together. Find someone who you feel this way about and who loves you the same way…with open arms…you will have ar amazing relationship. I believe you will have one of the greatest relationships in the history of humanity. This has been my experience.

On the contrary, when we have a verbal commitment to stay together forever, we jeopardize the passion that makes us want to commit in the first place. I believe that the moment we have a commitment, much of the magic and zest has disappears from the relationship. Moreover, when we have a commitment to remain together, it is human nature to start to take each other for granted. We are less likely to go out of our way to impress our partner, to flirt with our partner, or put as much effort into trying to attract our partner as we would *without* the commitment and the expectation that our partner will still be there tomorrow. We are less likely to put as much effort into trying to look good for each other because we've already "caught" our partner. By our nature, we like to pursue, and we like to be pursued. It's fun.

When there is no commitment, we don't take our partner for granted because we don't know how much time we will have together. It naturally drives us to make the most of every moment, and appreciate every moment together. When we truly enjoy the company of our partner, we want to keep spending time with that person, so we are naturally inclined to put more effort and more focus into the relationship to keep our partner happy. The lack of commitment naturally propels couples together, and leads to more enjoyment and satisfaction in the relationship.

There is another huge benefit with this arrangement that eliminates a huge stumbling block for a lot of couples: when we don't have a verbal commitment to stay together, it engenders an automatic, built-in trust for each other. The fact that our partner is free to go at any time, and yet is still there with us, eliminates all doubt about their affection…we know that they are right where they want to be. And our partner has the same certainty and trust, because they have granted us the same freedom. We don't have to wonder if our partner is cheating, or faking their love for fear of hurting us. There's no need to snoop, to see who our partner is texting; no need to get suspicious when they stay late at the office…. We each know that the other is there because they *want* to be there…not because of *an obligation* to be there. There is no need for cheating in this relationship because you are free each free to leave at any time, and still be loved as a friend. It's a beautiful thing when you know that that person would let you walk out the door and be with anyone else, and will still love you and care deeply for you.

From personal experience, I can tell you that this is an awesome relationship to have! This is the strongest bond that two people can have. Knowing that our partner loves us enough to let us go makes us cherish our partner, trust our partner, and of course we want to stay close to someone like that. Imagine the kind of passion and fun that could be experienced in a relationship like this. It frees us to love at the most intense level. Without strings. Without fear. 100%. Primitive love is meant for *right now*. We never know exactly how long it will last, and therefore cannot promise it into the future.

I also find that this attitude towards relationships…the uncertainty of the future…motivates us to use our time together more effectively, and with more intention. We spend our time *really* getting to find out about, discover, and experience that other person because you don't have an expectation of staying together for a lifetime. Perhaps for some people, they can stay happily together for a lifetime, but the key is to not have the *expectation* of staying happily together forever. **Adjusting the expectation, I believe, makes all the difference in how we approach our relationships and or breakups.**

Furthermore, if couples do decide to give marriage a shot, I hope that they won't be shocked when other people come into their lives that you will be extremely attracted to. In other words, you will likely fall in love again with someone else. Perhaps not with the intensity with which you fell for your spouse, but it will likely happen. I think this is one reason that the divorce rate is so high; people are surprised that their attraction to their spouse diminishes, and inevitably someone new comes along that they fall in love with. We might feel guilty for this as if it is some sort of betrayal to our spouse, or we may conclude that we married the wrong person, and this new person must be the one we were *actually* meant for. Even if we are steadfast and choose to remain faithful to our spouse, there are still going to be psychological consequences; there may still be feelings of guilt (for even having the attraction) and perhaps feelings of frustration for the lost opportunity and wondering what might have been.

I hope this helps explain why so many of us are so reluctant to get married. In my opinion, marriage goes against our nature----at least *part* of our nature: our evolved nature.

I don't see any benefit in making a commitment to stay together. On the contrary, I see all the benefits of *not* having a commitment; at least, not having a commitment to stay together for any amount of time. The kind of commitment that I think does make sense is a commitment to be honest with one another; to be genuine; to put our best effort into being present and pushing each other to grow; to try to enrich each other's lives for as long as we are together. I think it even makes sense to make a commitment that, even if the romance doesn't work out and we split up, we should commit to remaining friends after; no hard feelings. As mature adults, it is possible to do this.

To me, a healthy relationship (and really any relationship; even friends and family) fundamentally requires freedom. A relationship is a living thing; it needs air. It needs to breathe. The instant you have a commitment to stay together and never leave, it sucks all the air out of the relationship and it begins to wither and die. I have no doubt that some will want to cast stones at me for seeing it this way, and for saying so, but it is my honest opinion.

Chapter 16

Family

Many will ask how this new paradigm (no marriage/no commitment to stay together) works if two people are going to have children together. I understand the initial skepticism; but the new paradigm still works even with children in the picture. When we decide to raise children with our spouse or partner, we need to realize that we are still going to face all the challenges of maintaining healthy, successful relationships with our partner. Having children may serve to bring partners closer, but it will introduce new challenges to the relationship as well. Honestly, I think raising children together presents even *more* challenges to couples in order to maintain healthy, supportive, and fun relationships. The romance *and* the friendship will both be tested. Knowing that these challenges will come, we should be prepared to deal with them and work through them. If we decide that we are willing to endure those inevitable challenges that come in exchange for the joy and satisfaction of raising children together, then we stand a much better chance to function in our roles of partner and parent. I know this is a controversial statement, but I see no need for couples to get married, or commit to staying with one another *even if* they are going to have children together, for all the reasons that I have already laid out.

If we choose to have children with our partner, <u>there is a commitment we should make to one another:</u> **we should commit to raising the children as best as we can, regardless of how the relationship between the two of us evolves**. I think the agreement should be something like this, "Whether we remain together as a couple or not, we are going to commit to loving and raising these children to the best of our ability; as a team...even if the day comes when we are no longer happy together and split up as a romantic couple. Let's agree that our kids will always know their parents love them." To me, that is as much more realistic and noble commitment to make. This commitment puts the emphasis on the welfare of the children. Why is this preferable to the conventional wisdom that says we should get married? The reality is that married couples who have children together often realize they are not a healthy couple, and the kids often suffer the consequences of the failed romance. The home environment becomes toxic. When there is a divorce, the parents often resort to using the children as bargaining pieces to get back at one another. We also know that, often times after a divorce, one of the parents might completely abandon their role as parent and disappear because they harbor ill feelings toward their ex. This is a disaster. Once we choose to have children, we must understand that that children's health and happiness supersedes our own. We must decide that we will make those sacrifices. If we feel that it is important for parents to stay together in one household for the sake of the children, then we must understand that we will be sacrificing a lot of ourselves to make that happen peacefully. We must make these decisions consciously before having children, or as early as possible.

Whatever happens with the relationship between parents, the most important objective is to ensure the children have a healthy, loving upbringing. Whether the parents remain a couple or not, the children need to have parents who are involved and give them love and guidance. I reject the notion that it's *always* better for parents to remain together in the same household. Certainly when parents cannot get along, it is not preferable that they remain in the same household. I firmly believe that most of the sadness and trauma that children experience from their parents' divorce is a result of the pity that society heaps upon them because of it. Imagine how children reflexively feel from so many people echoing condolences such as: "I'm so sorry your parents are splitting up; "that's so sad; "that's too bad." Naturally, children internalize this negative energy, and assume that something *is* wrong…that divorce is something to be embarrassed about, or ashamed of, or something to feel bad about. What if we change the way we think about and talk about divorce? Why don't we be more honest about divorce? What if we say, "you know what, many couples get divorced"; "Your parents still care about each other, but it's difficult to make a marriage work"; "Divorce is almost always for the best"; "You'll be just fine"; …most importantly, "Your parents still love you, and will be there for you."

As a society, we must work to remove the stigma that is still associated with divorce. Divorce is neither shameful nor sad. It is simply two people being honest and recognizing that a relationship didn't work out. It's not uncommon. If two people aren't happy and fulfilled together, then divorce is great thing. I don't express pity to anyone about having gone through a divorce, because I realize that they are both in a better place. They may not realize it yet themselves, but I want to hasten their realization of this. They are now free to find a relationship that *does* work; that *is* fun; that *is* fulfilling.

If a couple wants to have kids, and both feel it is important to stay together in one household, I can understand that. We have been cultured to think that this is always the ideal family structure. Personally, I don't see any issue with raising children in two households, especially if the parents really can't get along under the same roof. It happens. Let's be real.

What is a family but **a group of people who love and take care of each other?** <u>**It is love that makes a family; not blood**</u>. In my parents' bathroom hangs a plaque that reads, "Friends are the family we choose for ourselves." I concur. It is the same love.

Change is requirement for survival. I believe that one of the conditions we accept from our Creator with the gift of life is to put some effort into making the world better: for ourselves, for our loved ones, for the world around us, and for future generations. We are not put on this Earth to mindlessly follow traditions; we are here to evolve and make progress toward greater freedom, greater equality, and bring more love into the world.

To me, the whole world is family. We should all care about and do our best to take care of each other. We need larger groups of people coming together in love to take care of and support each other. We should be expanding the definition of family rather than trying to limit it to a strict, traditional definition. By doing this the entire world would benefit.

Chapter 17

Forgiving

I hope that some will read this book and be inspired to try find it within them to forgive partners from their past; perhaps forgiving a spouse who left because they were no longer happy or even if they left for someone else. We are human beings, and we have to pursue happiness in this life while we are here. So many men and women get married before they truly know themselves, or truly know their spouse. Many people get married before they truly understand love. We've been raised under a false paradigm: that we would grow up, fall head over heels in love with "the one", get married and live happily ever after. But this is not the way love works. Is it fair to be upset with someone who made this discovery only after getting married? I hope that my perspectives and insights about human nature will help mend relationships and open men and women to forgiving their partners or former partners and healing emotional wounds.

I think it is a great shame that men and women that were so in love, or even married, oftentimes become bitter enemies when a relationship doesn't work out. No one goes through life trying to be a bad person. But many people are confused, and inadvertently cause pain and experience pain because of this confusion. Just because a

partner or spouse leaves to be with someone else, it doesn't mean they love that other person *more*. It simply means that they were a better match with someone else; they laugh more together and enjoy each other's conversation more, perhaps. There's no reason to feel any less about yourself, or to be upset with the other person. There's no crime here. Would anyone really ask their partner or spouse to stay with them out of pity, or an obligation, knowing that they would rather be with someone else? I don't see the logic of that.

The problem we have is "the promise" to stay together. Even when the promise to stay isn't spoken out loud, there seems to be an automatic implication of it when couples are dating. We need to stop that. I think it is much healthier to adopt an attitude of, "we're going to get to know about each other, and see if we make a good couple. If so, we will stay together for as long as the relationship is working for each of us---- as long as we have fun together and nurture each other in mind and spirit. But if the day comes that the relationship is no longer working, we will go our separate ways and still be friends, and still care about each other." In some ways, we are all still children learning about ourselves, learning about others, and learning how to love and relate to each other better.

Chapter 18

Love the World

When I speak of having "love for the world" or "loving everyone," this is a little different than "the deepest level of caring" that I've been describing. We can only obtain deepest level of caring by spending lots of quality time with someone, and getting to know, respect, and understand them intimately. Having love for the world is essentially just a having a basic level of caring about people---- about humanity. I think it's vitally important to keep it in your heart and mind to simply wish people well, to hold hope for them to be free from suffering and oppression, want them to be happy and free, want their children to be happy and free and have opportunities to live great lives. When we love the world we want people to have food and water, to have economic opportunity, perhaps most importantly, to have **hope** for a better future for themselves and their loved ones. I firmly believe that when people have hope for themselves and their loved ones...no one wants to go to war.

These are the wishes that I have for everyone, everywhere. I don't care what country someone is in, or what their religion or biases are...I want people to be happy and hopeful. I think most of us feel this way, but **let's try to think it more often and say it once in a while!** Let's say it to ourselves and say it to each other. Let's reflect on that love of common humanity constantly. If humanity is going to survive and thrive then we have to mature and realize that "love of country" isn't going to cut it any longer. It's too small-minded. More and more of us *must* start thinking in terms of "love of humanity" and act in accordance with that love. We must let it be known to our political leaders that we want policies that do more to address the plight of people *around the world.* Our survival depends on it; we are all connected. How many medical and scientific breakthroughs could we make if we invested in the healthcare and education of children around the world? Every person on this planet has gifts and talents to share with the world, but they need healthcare, food, and education to bring those gifts to light. These are investments that **always** pays dividends. It's a no-brainer.

Love your neighbor as yourself.

—Mark 12:31

I have critiqued many of the clichés surrounding love, but here is a cliché I have no problem with: "Love conquers all." I believe love can and will conquer all, but let's be clear: it's not the primitive version of love between sexual partners that will conquer the problems that face humanity and the world; it is the evolved version of love that will save us, and propel humanity to the next phase of our evolution— lasting peace and prosperity, equality, and freedom for all. When all of humanity starts investing in one another's healthcare, education, and economic opportunity, we will finally find a cure to cancer and extend human life span by leaps and bounds; we can finally put an end to poverty, hunger, and war. But each of us must take it upon ourselves to consciously summon the love, to bring it into the world through acts of kindness and contribution to the common good. We must strive to do great things and inspire others to do likewise. It is in this evolved version of love that we find heaven and feel 'complete'; not romantic love.

Conclusion

I hope my book helps to shed some light on these complicated concepts, helps to free people from their fear, helps people to recover from past hurts, and will help the world to improve how we love each other. We are here in this life to connect to others. We cannot connect if we are not open. We cannot be fully open unless we conquer our fear. I hope my insights and philosophies will be helpful to people, whether they agree with my ultimate conclusions about marriage and commitment. Each of us must take the time to contemplate what it means to love, and what our expectations are going to be. Even if you disagree with everything I say, I sincerely hope that understanding my perspective will help solidify your own.

Over the past few years, as my concepts were crystallizing, I would often discuss my views with close friends. On more than one occasion they would ask, "Doug, don't you think you're going against human nature?" To which I would reply, "yes, I am going against our *primitive* nature, but my point is marriage and possessiveness go against our *evolved* nature."

"Which wolf will win?"

The elder simply replied, "The one you feed."

We must decide individually, and decide as a species, which part of our nature we will feed: the primitive, selfish nature that wants to possess those we love, or the evolved, compassionate, altruistic nature that, above all else, wants those we love to be happy.

Afterword

I wrote the rough draft to this book several years ago, but I lacked confidence in my writing ability and therefore did not seek to publish it right away. I assumed someone else would come along and point out these same observations, and do it more convincingly. But I now realize that's not how life works. If you have something to say, even if it's similar to someone else's perspective, it's still worth sharing your own unique perspective for the chance that it might help someone else. The reality is that we all have different perspectives, and we've learned different lessons from our personal struggles. We should all feel free to share our thoughts and perspectives, and we should encourage one another to share our perspectives in effort to help others on their journey through life. Rest assured: somebody out there needs to hear what you have to say.

If there's some desire burning inside you, something you want to tell the world, then I strongly encourage you to raise your voice; write a book; start a blog; start a YouTube channel. Do not let your self-esteem, or ego, or your satisfaction hinge upon how many people read or are affected by it. In Rudyard Kipling's classic poem "If," there is a couplet that reads, "if you can meet with Triumph and Disaster and treat those two imposters just the same...." what matters is the *attempt* to help others, to contribute, to open yourself to the world, and the effort you exert in the process.

I honestly believe that we all have things to learn from each other, and with the technology we have in the modern world to communicate with each other, I see huge potential for tremendous progress across the globe. We should all feel free to speak our minds, even if our ideas go against custom—perhaps even more so if they go against custom.

Humanity's great task is not simply to follow custom and tradition; but rather to examine our customs and traditions, and, where there is room for improvement, to change, to make progress, and to evolve. If we had always blindly followed traditions in the United States, women would still not have the right to vote, and we'd still have slavery in the South. There are many more changes to society that we have a responsibility to work toward. Don't get me wrong, we should take the time to play, to dance, and to party in life, but we must also do our work to continue humanity's march toward equality, freedom, peace, and love. Change is necessary for growth, and for survival; not just on an individual level, but as a societal level as well. This is a dark hour for humanity. So many of us seem to have forgotten that life is about connection to others and working with others toward a better future. But let us remember that it is always darkest before the dawn. Let us commit ourselves to a worldwide wake-up and finally put an end to our myopia and recognize our unity with every other person and our shared destiny. We're either going to sink or thrive together. Let us usher in a new age of love, peace, and prosperity to all.

Made in the USA
Lexington, KY
20 August 2019